they, by the
tion, replaced
and fed by s
The Menace (
bodiment of this heritage is now symbolized
by an organization known as Protestants and
Other Americans United for Separation of
Church and State; more briefly, in initials,
P.O.A.U.

But from the beginning sincere men of
good will strove to overcome their private
prejudices in their public utterances and
policies. Roger Williams, founder of Rhode
Island, imposed no prohibition to Catholic
Faith or ceremonies. And William Penn,
founder of Pennsylvania, opened the way
for the Church to emerge from the catacombs of private homes to the light of semi-
public worship.

When the Declaration of Independence
was signed there was hardly a Catholic
church in the colonies able to have public
worship for the 5,000 Catholics. A century
later there were 5,000 churches for some
6,000,000 Catholics.

Through the efforts of sincere men on both
sides we have seen public opinion change
and we are able to record the progressive
liquidation of the inherited animosity of four
centuries. The Catholic's fellow-countrymen
have at last gotten beyond the conception
they have formed of the Roman Catholic
Church. *The Catholic In America* will do
much to enable them to see the Church as
she is.

The history and deeds of *The Catholic In
America* and the words of the Church's hierarchy can hardly be clearer in stating the
Church's intentions. But neither words nor
deeds will convince those who refuse to be
convinced. Nevertheless, history, deeds and
statements constitute an unequivocal commitment to the principle of the equality of
all religions before the civil law. On that
commitment American Catholics stood and
stand.

THE CATHOLIC
IN AMERICA

THE CATHOLIC IN AMERICA

From Colonial Times to the Present Day

by

Peter J. Rahill, Ph.D.

FRANCISCAN HERALD PRESS
Publishers of Franciscan Literature
Chicago 9, Illinois

FOREWORD

At the ceremony at which Mother Seton was declared Venerable, our Holy Father, Pope John XXIII, made the observation that the Church in the United States had grown greatly since that distant day when Mother Seton lived. He went on to say that Catholicism in the United States has, "passed its time of development and now approaches full maturity." The flowering of the bloom of Faith in our country as hailed by Our Holy Father is something that brings joy to the hearts of all of us. However, we would be blind to reality if we did not know that there were many storms along the way of our history to hinder and disturb the growth of the Church in our country.

In the pages of this book, Father Rahill has rendered a great service in showing for us the Church in its humble beginnings, at times weak and almost powerless against the onslaught of bigotry. But, at the same time, demonstrating evidence of the sturdiness that was displayed as it withstood the blows which would seem to ruin it. There is delineated for us the step by step process which the Church used in overcoming obstacles along the way and bringing it to the point where it is now enjoying the warm sun of God's beneficence.

The author has taken a good honest look at the trials which have come to the Church in America. He does not minimize the difficulties encountered, but it is with gratifying comfort that we learn in this book of the steady reduction in the violence of bigotry. Periods of relative tranquillity were disrupted by flashes of religious partisanship, but that discord persistently, if not uniformly, lessened with the passage of years. In this respect it may truly be asserted that all Americans have developed and matured together. In the presentation of this graph lies the principal worth of this account.

7

From this sight of the long road already traveled with ever increasing ease, may everyone be inspired to strive mightily for complete harmony among all Americans.

During all the centuries of the life of the Universal Church, she has always been beset by squalls and storms. One would indeed be naive if the present improved situation in our country is interpreted as the arrival of the millennium. It is nonetheless a matter of enormous satisfaction to realize that the Bark of Peter is riding seas that are high but in no sense perilous as far as our own country is concerned.

It seems significant to observe that American Catholics can make a great contribution to the further reduction of ill will in our land by striving to possess the maturity about which the Holy Father spoke. The mature man is the peaceful man. In this sense, peace does not mean inactivity or lassitude, but quite the opposite. It is a peace that is filled with charity, with justice and a desire to promote both of these even as Christ would have us do. By its very excellence, this maturity will inspire imitation and attract all men to follow the same path.

The Catholic in America is a book that can only promote "understanding." It should be read and absorbed and passed on from Catholic reader to non-Catholic friend. It is concise. Compact. Factual. Dispassionate. It is a simple and sober summary of the history of the Catholic Church in America from Colonial times to our own days.

To know our history is to know human nature with its emotions and its prejudices and its bigotry. It is to understand that though knowledge is necessary, charity is paramount. Though differences are great, the scandal is not our failure to agree, but our failure to love.

† Leo C. Byrne
Auxiliary Bishop of Saint Louis

CONTENTS

THE CATHOLIC
IN AMERICA

Chapter I

WHY DOES HOSTILITY TO
AMERICAN CATHOLICS PERSIST?

WHY DO PEOPLE HOLD MY CATHOLICITY AGAINST ME? THANK GOD, the question does not arise every day in the life of an American Catholic. But it will be asked by the man who was passed over for promotion when his religion was apparently or openly the decisive factor. A woman will be dismayed at the tension sensed in a social gathering when she announces her membership in the Church. Even those who have no personal affronts are reminded daily that the question is being asked.

ANIMOSITY LESSENS

Both consolation and strength come from the knowledge that this is not an affliction peculiar to our own day. A century and a quarter ago Bishop John England declared that a deadly hostility existed in many places against Catholics. Then an acknowledged spokesman for the Church in the United States, the Bishop of Charleston warned that "in denouncing Catholicity throughout the length and breadth of the land, there is found a common ground upon which the discordant camps can meet and bend in amity."

Resistance as well as forbearance will come from greater familiarity with what has been successfully surmounted in the past.

13

Immediately it should be noted that the position of Catholics has improved vastly during the years; conversely animosity toward members of the Church has lessened. Present charges of double allegiance, subjection to a foreign power, and unfitness of Catholic candidates for high office are irritating. But they do not foment the heat inherent in these epithets heard by Bishop England and his fellow Catholics: "Papists," "Popery," and "priest-ridden!"

Sometimes well-meaning individuals express admiration for the Church's doctrines but decry the authority of the Pope. They laud her strong influence for good but bemoan the existence of her hierarchy. Such praise is no praise! From the first it should be understood that no actual favor is tendered by making an invalid distinction. In establishing His Church Jesus Christ selected Peter and the other Apostles to guide and lead its members. A body without a head is a corpse; our loyal defense is of a living Church!

Today "dialogue" is popular both as a word and as an aspiration. Expressed thus or simply as conversation it becomes increasingly fruitful as the speakers are well-informed. Hence this review of the trials and triumphs of the Church in the United States is intended primarily to provide additional knowledge for "over-the-fence" talks. On the bus or at the club, after the farmers' co-op meeting or from the backyard to a neighbor, a Catholic will help the Church and himself by being better informed about her.

Were differences merely imaginary there would be no need for this account. Yet the common ground which exists for those inside and out of the Church is far broader than many realize. A hundred million and more Americans profess religious affiliation. The great majority are Christians, and thus all of them profess belief in Jesus Christ. Moreover, virtually all are spiritual descendants of God's Chosen People. Accordingly the common ground is broadened farther to encompass Jews as well as Christians. But why do so many entertain suspicions, if not hostility, toward us Catholics?

PROTESTANT REVOLT

The principal divisive factor unquestionably was the Protestant Revolt of the 16th century. Mistaken though the leaders were in quitting their ancestral fold, recent Catholic writers have softened the harshness of prior judgments of them as individuals. For its part the Presbyterian Church, U.S.A., has stricken from its creed the traditional damning of the Pope as "anti-Christ." The findings of scholars, however, are long delayed in reaching the masses of people. Meanwhile doubts and distrust of Catholics by their neighbors do not vanish.

To exaggerated nationalism may be attributed much of the blame. Love of country is indeed a virtue but — in the words of Theodore Roosevelt — "no man is a true American who hates another country more than he loves his own." All Christendom recognizing the Pope as supreme head gave way to political sectioning embittered by religious friction. Often unjustified, popular fancy persisted in fashioning credal molds for nations or peoples. A North German or Scandinavian was presumed to be Lutheran, while a Frenchman or a Spaniard must belong to the Catholic Church.

Geography preserved the separation for three long centuries. In this era of jet mobility it is difficult to realize that most people never ventured more than walking distance from the place they were born. Misbeliefs about distant and unseen Catholics assumed the rigidity of the language spoken or the number of furrows to an acre.

HOSTILITY INHERITED

In Scotland the extermination of Catholicism was much more complete than it ever was in England. Conformance to the church established by Henry VIII never approached total realization, and there were Catholics during the darkest days of suppression. The valiant Catholics who persevered were not considered allies by the multiple English dissenters. With their own opponents within the Anglican Church these separatists found — to repeat the words of Bishop England about the United States — "a common ground upon which the discordant camps can meet and bend in amity."

Physicists teach that a certain amount of heat or energy is lost in transmission. Not so with Old World animosity toward Catholics! That it was frequently intensified rather than reduced or mitigated will be seen in later chapters. Even to this day the consequences are felt. The eminent Jesuit, John Courtney Murray, has said that we are all in some way the product of our histories. Red hair or blue eyes may be ours from an unknown great-grandfather. Likewise the hostility expressed by some fellow-American may have been unwittingly inherited by him. Oftentimes today's anti-Catholicism originated in a long-forgotten mesalliance of exaggerated nationalism and hostility to the ancestral Church.

Fortitude and patience are not contradictory virtues, and the American Catholic of the 1960's may have frequent occasion to call upon his reserve of both qualities. Because of the possibility of personal advantage, statements by living figures of whatever prominence may not be accepted readily by those outside the Church. It is heartening, then, to recall the profession of faith of a churchman who was outstanding in both the 19th and in the 20th centuries. Himself an immigrant, Archbishop John Ireland uttered the words which all American Catholics are proud to repeat today. Lacking only the music of his powerful voice, the words ring forth as: "My religious faith is that of the Catholic Church — Catholicism, integral and unalloyed, unswerving and soul-swaying. . . . My civil and political faith is that of the Republic of the United States — Americanism, truest and brightest, yielding in strength and loyalty to the Americanism of none other American."

Chapter II

EUROPEAN ENMITY TO CATHOLICS TRANSMITTED TO THE ENGLISH COLONIES

A UNIVERSAL CHRISTENDOM UNDER THE SUZERAINTY OF THE Pope was shattered by the Protestant Revolt. Not that this ideal of the Middle Ages had ever been fully realized. But the goal of the future was wrecked completely on the shoals of private ambitions and exaggerated nationalism. Venerable Carlton J. H. Hayes, the convert historian, has expressed well the contrary spirit. In one of his many essays he pointed out that anti-Catholicism has chiefly been based upon the inherent dread Protestantism has for the supranational influence which radiates from Rome.

ELIZABETH I

To no one country or religion was the antagonism limited. And most Americans today, much less the Catholics among them, do not claim English ancestry. Notwithstanding, particular attention must be given to England because the colonies along the Atlantic seaboard were under her rule and laws. In the mother country that had meant outright persecution of Catholics almost immediately from the accession of Elizabeth I in 1558. Reneging on her promise to Mary Tudor to remain a Catholic, the new queen militantly espoused the Anglican Church established by her father, Henry VIII.

Not especially attractive personally but certainly efficient, Elizabeth quickly brought both church and state under the sway of her scepter. The Act of Supremacy of 1559 completely out- lawed the Catholic Church, to which the majority of Englishmen still belonged. Elizabeth's excommunication by Pope Pius V had a negative result. Though most Catholics never wavered in their loyalty to the crown, they became "second-class citizens" in the eyes of their fellow men. They were further stigmatized as a group by John Foxe's *Book of Martyrs*. Now fully discredited, for sev- eral centuries this single book caused thousands of English readers to detest Catholics.

For opposite reasons two groups in England came to oppose Elizabeth. The Puritans wanted to purify Anglicanism of "the trap- pings of Popery." The Separatists, on the other hand, objected not to the ceremonial but to the church being ruled by the Queen. The Pilgrims who landed at Plymouth in 1620 were a division of the Separatists, or Independents. Soon they were followed and grad- ually absorbed by the larger group of Puritans. The New England settlers were not of a common religious cause with those in the first successful English foundation at Jamestown. There the Established Church was accepted without discussion and no concern expressed for nonexistent Catholics.

DEATH PENALTY

The Massachusetts Bay Colony was equally destitute of Cath- olics. But "No Popery" from the very first acted as a cohesive in- fluence for the settlers. The severity of treatment experienced by Hester Prynne, as conceived by Nathaniel Hawthorne, today appalls many readers. But her scarlet letter was mild compared with the tortures proposed for any Catholics venturing into the colony. Prosperity came to replace theology as the primary concern of the New Englanders. Yet the imprecations against the Catholic Church and her members increased rather than lessened.

Far to the north Samuel de Champlain had founded Quebec in 1608. Being both French and Catholics, these people were considered enemies by the Puritans. As early as 1647 death was the penalty prescribed for offering Mass or even for the presence of a priest in the area controlled by the Massachusetts Bay Colony. Three years later a curious relaxation occurred in the rigor of this law. An Indian missionary, Father Gabriel Druillettes, came down the Kennebec River to propose an alliance of the English with the French against the Iroquois Indians. Not only was the priest cordially received, but in the home of Governor William Bradford he was served fish on Friday. Though the missionary returned a year later, no league was effected. Yet temporarily self-preservation had triumphed over hatred of Catholicism among the Puritans.

The colony of Maryland will be treated in the next chapter. It should be noted here that the presence of Catholics on Chesapeake Bay aroused the anti-Catholicism of their neighbors to the south. Virginia imitated Massachusetts Bay in fierce enactments against Catholics. A "Papist" was even prohibited from owning a horse valued at more than five pounds. Apparently this statute had only a nuisance value, but it is indicative of the calculated antipathy for members of the Catholic Church. A colony was successfully established in the Carolinas under Charles II. Though the King was at least sympathetic to Catholics from the beginning of his reign, the Church of England was established by law. Hence no inducement existed for Catholics to emigrate here nor to Georgia in the next century. Protestant dissenters were permitted in both colonies, but the liberty thus granted specifically excluded "Papists."

HATRED PERSISTS

The bitterness of anti-Catholicism was not mellowed by the passage of a century and more. Almost 150 years after the settlement at Jamestown, the Acadians were deported from Nova Scotia. Because of war with France the actions could be labeled political and military. But the dire consequences suffered by the exiles were due to their known Catholicity. No sanctuary would be granted them as they drifted southward in their boats. Refuge finally was found in the bayous of Louisiana. Evangeline had a Longfellow to lament her heartbreak. How many more Gabriels were there who searched for their loved ones in vain?

Catholics did fight in the American Revolution. To explain how they existed at all until 1776, separate treatment will be given to the colonies of Maryland and Pennsylvania particularly. Monsignor Peter Guilday, late historian of the Church in the United States, contended that the War of Independence saved the few colonial Catholics from complete extermination. Though the freedom gained was neither complete nor immediate, the vise of intolerance never again came so near to closing on the very bone and blood of American Catholics.

Chapter III

MARYLAND: SANCTUARY AND THEN PRISON FOR CATHOLICS

MORE BITTER THAN HER FATHER, HENRY VIII, AND DETERMINED to protect her position as sovereign, Elizabeth I of England used every possible means of suppressing her Catholic subjects. Torture and death on the scaffold were physical barbarities suffered by many. Virtually all were afflicted by the fines imposed for failure to attend the Anglican religious services. In the later 1500's the jails and prisons became so overcrowded with impoverished Catholics that the local officials begged the Queen to send no more.

THE ONLY REFUGE

Thus Elizabeth was faced with a double dilemma, for she did not want to exile wealthy and influential Catholics. Consequently, the Act of 1593 prohibited them from leaving the homeland. On the other hand, those who had no more than a pittance or less were urged to quit the kingdom. This same law made it treasonable for them to go to the continent. With all Europe closed, the New World was the only possible refuge for persecuted Catholics.

As early as 1583, both as sponsors and as emigrants, Catholics participated in an expedition under Sir Humphrey Gilbert. In a disaster off the coast of Maine immigrants perished together with Catholic hopes of an American refuge. While a few of the faithful participated in other ventures, the failure of these attempts caused the 16th century to pass with no settlement for them opened in the New World.

Not one of the old Catholic families but a convert furnished the means and the leadership of the first and only successful Catholic settlement. As a graduate of Oxford, it was after James I had succeeded Elizabeth that George Calvert returned from a tour of the continent. From James Catholics had hoped for toleration because of his own Catholic background. But to further his own ambitions, James had acquiesced in the execution of his mother, the romantic Mary Stuart. Any consideration he may have entertained for the expectantly eager Catholics vanished from the moment of the discovery of the unfortunate Gunpowder Plot to blow up the King and Parliament.

George Calvert already was high in the favor of the King. Like St. Paul, he then participated in the persecution of the Catholics he later joined. He was promoted to Secretary of State; in appreciation of his service James knighted him and bestowed a large estate in Ireland. All this royal preferment Lord Baltimore — the title which had come to Calvert — risked in order to embrace the Catholic Faith. Fortunately the friendship of the King was retained. Calvert, however, resigned as Secretary of State because he could no more take the oath of office than one of the early Catholics could offer incense before a statue of the Roman Emperor.

CHARLES GRANTS CHARTER

In 1627 Calvert sailed with Catholic and Protestant colonists for Newfoundland. Early in 1629 Lady Baltimore and their children followed. Newfoundland was considered attractive because of being closer to Europe and of the same latitude, but the climate proved too rigorous for the colony to endure. Going southward, Baltimore was brusquely refused admission to Virginia because of his religion. To return to England for a second attempt was his only hope.

James I had died but his son, Charles, was equally friendly to the Calverts. To Lord Baltimore the King granted a charter for settlement on both sides of Chesapeake Bay, stipulating that the colony was to be named Maryland after Henrietta Marie, the French Catholic who was his Queen.

Perhaps worn out by his exertions overseas, Lord Baltimore died at this very time. Long delay or disaster could have been the fate of Catholic aspirations. But Charles I confirmed the grant to the Baron's oldest son, Cecil. The second Lord Baltimore, like his father a zealous Catholic convert, proceeded with the plans for a settlement in the New World. Reflecting the struggles of Charles I with a recalcitrant Parliament, the charter was a unique document in two ways. First, all power in the colony was vested in Lord Baltimore. "Monarch of all he surveyed" was true of Cecil Calvert within the confines of the grant. Moreover, by the fourth section of the charter Catholics had a refuge for the first time since Elizabeth I ascended the throne of England some 70 years before.

As his father had done for the venture to Newfoundland, Cecil Calvert made the colony open to all, Catholic and non-Catholic. Before they departed he warned his coreligionists against giving offense by word or deed to those not of the Faith. Such caution was wise. Once the project had become known violent protests spewed forth. Those opposing the sailing openly declared the fervor of Protestants would disappear if there were no Catholics in England to hunt down. If wry humor be permitted, the faithful then might be compared to a dog track where without the electric rabbit the hounds would cease to run.

FIRST MASS

But Cecil Calvert was as sturdy and unyielding as his father. Despite rantings and threats the *Ark* and the *Dove* bravely sailed forth and the perilous voyage across the Atlantic was completed successfully. The first Mass in the Maryland colony was celebrated by Father Andrew White on the Feast of the Annunciation, 1634. Lord Baltimore appointed his brother, Leonard, Governor of the colony. Friendly relations were established with the Indians and it was not from the red men that attacks came. Armed forays were made against the new settlement by neighboring Virginians. Dangerous though these were, it was from within that the greater danger gradually arose.

Maryland was intended to be a Catholic refuge but, as has been noted, immigration to the colony was not limited to the faithful. Nor was there any restriction once settlement was successfully established. Wrangling already had broken out among the Puritans in America and nonconformists were expelled from the Massachusetts Bay Colony. These and others found a haven on Chesapeake Bay. Rather than laboring under restrictions, some of these exiles actually were protected from Catholic aggression. In the first years two heavy fines were exacted from Catholic settlers who had violated the freedom guaranteed to Protestants. The sanctuary of Catholics became the refuge of dissenters among the Puritans. Too soon it was the Catholics who were to suffer from this charitable hospitality.

The colony had prospered during the 13 years that Leonard Calvert was governor. At his death, however, non-Catholics far outnumbered the faithful and Lord Baltimore was forced to appoint a Protestant governor. In 1649 the Maryland Assembly passed its justly renowned Toleration Act. This celebrated statute provided for religious freedom for every Christian! Catholics may take everlasting pride that a commencement of religious freedom in the United States originated from the faithful in the colony of Maryland.

SEVERE PENAL LAWS

Dissenters of every variety, therefore, had full rights with the Catholic founders. Soon the givers were to be excluded from the enjoyment of the freedom granted. About five years later Catholicity actually was outlawed in the colony. "No Popery" resounded as loudly and vehemently on the Chesapeake as it had in the Puritan Commonwealth of Massachusetts.

After the death of Oliver Cromwell and the restoration of the Stuarts in England, the colony was returned to Lord Baltimore. Nonetheless, until the American Revolution freedom for the faithful in Maryland was precarious. At times restrictions were relaxed; again the largest body of Catholics in the English colonies were subjected to severe penal laws. A century later Maryland enacted legislation which weighed down all property owned by Catholics with double taxation. Catholics of 18th-century Maryland actually considered quitting the colony entirely to make a new start in French Louisiana. Only on the outbreak of colonial disagreement with the mother country prior to the Revolution was this proposal postponed. But Maryland, the Land of Sanctuary, had become a prison for the faithful. Whether shouted by Puritans or by Anglicans, "No Popery" was the cry in command. Toleration was forgotten, religious freedom had been blotted out on the statute books of the English colonies in America.

Chapter IV

PENNSYLVANIA AFFORDED CATHOLICS FREEDOM OUTSIDE THE LAW

IN ENGLAND PENAL LAWS AGAINST CATHOLICS WERE BY NO means abolished after the death of Elizabeth I in 1603. Many pulpits in both mother country and colonies joined the Anglican divine John Tillotson in invectives against "the restless and black designs of that sure and inveterate Enemy of ours, the Church of Rome." In America the response had been legal proscription of Catholics save in Maryland. There the charity of the founders to those outside the Faith ultimately cost Catholics their American sanctuary.

ROGER WILLIAMS

In the colonial desert of anti-Catholicism Pennsylvania came to be the single oasis where the green stalk of the Faith could be cultivated in relative freedom. Before reviewing the origin and endurance of this liberty a salute is due to a pioneer American apostle of creedal equality. His name is by no means unknown; he was Roger Williams. Because his fairness had virtually no effect on colonial Catholics it would be easy to neglect his contribution.

Williams was born in Wales a half dozen years prior to the birth of the first son of George Calvert, originator of the colony of

26

Maryland. During the last years of the long reign of Elizabeth the Queen forced conformity among the Welsh to her Established Church. After Williams graduated from Cambridge, he became an Anglican divine. But his prompt disagreement with the state religion made his exodus to America a salutary move for him. Landing in Boston in 1631, he was soon in disfavor akin to that previously suffered in the mother country. Roger Williams' Puritanism was not identical with that of the leaders in New England. Unlike them, having come to America for his own religious freedom he advocated lifting any restrictions on the consciences of others.

Again departing hastily rather than conforming, Williams founded Providence in Rhode Island. There he followed Calvert in time at least in his grant of religious freedom to all Christians. Probably no Catholics were in his colony during his lifetime, but the lack of mention of "Papists" may not be ascribed to inadvertence on the part of Williams. In fact, more credit is due to him for his charity in that his private letters disclosed his personal hostility to the Catholic Church. Notwithstanding his hatred of a religion he did not know as it is in truth, Williams imposed no prohibition to Catholic Faith or ceremonies. While today Rhode Island has the highest percentage of Catholics of any state, virtually none found haven in the colony. After 1728 Catholics were completely disfranchised by the Assembly of Rhode Island and that discrimination continued after the American Revolution.

WILLIAM PENN

Pennsylvania was the sole English colony in America to be named after its actual founder. Distinguished for many attributes, William Penn resembled Roger Williams in suppressing his personal hostility in his public utterances relative to Catholicism. Then, too, he was like George Calvert. In the first legislation for his colony in 1682 Penn incorporated both civil and religious

equality for all as Calvert had in Maryland. "On Religion" was
the title of the initial chapter of this "Great Law." Therein it was
stated that all persons "living in this Province . . . shall not in any
case be molested or prejudiced for his, or her, conscientious per-
suasion or practice." A few Catholics who came in the first years
found these words verified by an actual welcome. Despite his fellowship with the Quakers, Penn enjoyed royal favor in the court
of the Stuarts, Charles II and James II. The collapse of the reign
of James II, England's last Catholic king, threatened to involve
William Penn in the upheaval. The proprietor hurried back to
England to protect his interests; he succeeded. After several years
the new Protestant regime confirmed his title and Penn returned
to America.

On the accession of William and Mary the British Parliament
had proclaimed the Toleration Act of 1689. Thereby restrictions
were removed from all dissenters save the beleaguered adherents
to the original Christianity, Catholics. The Test Oath exacted from
all officeholders had been condemned long before by Pope Paul
VII in 1607. In his native land and in his colony Penn resisted this
inclusion of the denial of Transubstantiation in the Mass. To retain
his proprietorship he eventually had to yield. Prodded by Parliament hostile to everything Catholic, the last of the Stuarts, Queen
Anne, ordered incorporation of the Test Oath in the qualification
of every office holder. With this bar to any participation by the
faithful in the government of the colony, legal freedom for Catholics vanished in Pennsylvania until 1776.

MASS IN PHILADELPHIA

Anti-Catholicism was present in Pennsylvania during the 18th
century. Still, the constitutional ban on Catholics was not fashioned
into a club of religious persecution. A surreptitious manner of
operation, however, had the expected consequence of very sketchy

records by Catholics themselves. Hence it is from a letter of protest by a Protestant minister named John Talbot that it is known a Mass was publicly offered in Philadelphia around 1708. While William Penn wrote to the governor from England, apparently no oppressive action was taken.

As opposition intensified in the once Catholic foundation of Maryland, the border between these two colonies and the present Delaware was the scene of much Catholic activity. Any increase in efforts at suppression could thereby be met by a quick shift in the place where Mass was offered, where one of the proscribed priests lived, or the site of one of the sporadic attempts at giving Catholic education. In 1711 there were nine priests near this "friendly Pennsylvania line." From this point they attended the faithful in these three colonies. Frequent excursions into New York were made by one or other of the priests.

German and Irish immigrants added to the Catholic population. Then, too, the continued toleration beyond or outside the law emboldened the faithful. This continued after their original protector, William Penn, had died in England in 1718. With St. Joseph as its patron, a church finally was opened in Philadelphia in 1734. As may be seen today, it was built on a side street (Willing's Alley). Thus attracting little attention, it was not a source of constant irritation to hostile eyes. With the erection of St. Joseph's it could be said that the Church — even though still outside the law — had emerged from the catacombs of private homes at least to the light of semi-public worship. In 1774 the future President John Adams reported visiting a "Romish chapel," which was St. Joseph's.

TENSION LESSENS

A generation of peace between France and England in the Old World and the New was reflected in tranquility for Catholicism in Pennsylvania. The cry of "No Popery" was raised afresh when hostilities were resumed between these major European powers and their allies. While active persecution was missing, the loyalty of Catholic colonists was questioned anew. "Papists" were forbidden to settle in western Pennsylvania where they would be proximate to the enemy under the Lilies of France. The Treaty of Paris of 1763 removed the proximate military danger from either France or Spain. That lessened if it did not eliminate the tension under which Pennsylvania Catholics lived.

During the French and Indian War a census of the Catholics in the colony of William Penn reckoned their number as 1,374. How minute was this little band in comparison with Pennsylvania's total population of approximately a half million! That the most rabid anti-Catholic would be concerned with so scanty a minority is difficult to understand today. Yet the fulminations of the Puritans in New England against "the Papists" was at its height in 1687 when a French traveler reported finding "eight or ten Catholics" in Boston! Clearly outside the law, Catholics in Pennsylvania nonetheless enjoyed the greatest freedom of all the faithful along the Atlantic seaboard. Though few in number, from them came the leaders of the Church once the new nation was formed. Hence it is not to Lord Baltimore alone, but to Roger Williams and even more to William Penn that Catholics are indebted for having survived colonial anti-Catholicism.

Chapter V

ENGLISH REVOLUTION INTENSIFIED COLONIAL ANTI-CATHOLICISM

NO ALL-PERVADING LIGHT — NONETHELESS, ONE MORE STAR OF liberty gleamed amid the gloom of colonial anti-Catholicism. While this instance is to the credit of all Americans, Catholics may take pride that the religious freedom was granted by a Catholic colonial governor. Moreover, the freedom of conscience was extended to everyone. A brief tribute is deserved by Colonel Thomas Dongan, Governor of the Province of New York from 1682 to 1688.

THOMAS DONGAN

Born in Ireland the same year that the colony of Maryland was founded (1634), Thomas Dongan was related to the Calverts by marriage. When King Charles I was beheaded by the Puritans, the Dongan family left England for France. Thomas rose to the rank of colonel in a regiment of Irish exiles fighting for France. Notwithstanding, he obeyed an order issued by Charles II for all Englishmen to return home.

The Duke of York, brother of Charles II, was proprietor of the colony which had been named after him. As is well known, the original settlement on Manhattan Island had been made by the

Dutch. In turmoil from the time of its seizures by the English, New York quickly responded to Dongan's wise rule. The action which rendered his administration completely distinctive was taken almost as soon as he assumed control.

In 1683 Dongan convoked the first representative assembly in the history of New York Province. "A Charter of Liberties" was adopted at the instigation of the Governor. The title of the legislation was fully merited by its provisions. Patrick Henry's rallying call was anticipated in the stipulation that there was to be no taxation without representation. Equally unique and more apropos to our discussion, religious liberty was given to all residents. On receiving the document in London, the Board of Trade and Plantations vetoed the legislation. Nothwithstanding, toleration continued during Dongan's term of office.

Bankruptcy and persecution were the Governor's personal return for his advanced legislation. With the accession of William and Mary to the English throne, Dongan was in complete disfavor as a Catholic and a favorite of the Stuarts. Though he became Earl of Limerick on the death of his brother, Thomas died in obscure poverty.

WILLIAM OF ORANGE

Dongan's charter has been called the "Magna Charta of American Constitutional Liberties." How surprising it is to find some historians almost ignoring it. With the Protestant ascendancy complete in the mother country, the New York Assembly promptly nullified all of Dongan's liberality. Once again the Catholic Church was outlawed and legislators fulminated against "the diabolical designs of the wicked and cruel Papists." Over and over again during the 18th century many of the provisions of Dongan's charter were petitioned for from the mother country. But religious liberty for Catholics was not one of them. The American Revolution came and succeeded, but rights were not restored to Catholics until 1806.

It would be misleading to leave the impression that the reversal of policy in New York was peculiar to that province alone. All of the colonies had been markedly affected by a revolution in the mother country. The Catholic James II had been replaced by William and Mary, the latter a Protestant daughter of the departing sovereign. The new King, William of Orange, has been called the "idol of 17th century Protestantism." He readily dropped the Calvinism of the Netherlands for the Established Church of England. Parliament, now supreme rather than the King, passed the "Toleration Act of 1689," whereby freedom was granted to all of the dissenting Protestant sects. Catholics, however, were specifically excluded from the indulgence. Further legislation in 1701 stipulated that no Catholic could succeed to the English throne, a prohibition which endures to this day.

In the American colonies, as in the mother country, dissenters no longer had any reason of self-preservation for making common cause with Catholics. Thus was halted the trend, minor though it had been, of the faithful enjoying any better treatment in the colonies than in England. Until the revolution in England in 1689 the substantial number of Catholics in Maryland, as well as the attempts of Roger Williams, William Penn, and Thomas Dongan to give freedom of conscience to all seemed to indicate that the hostility to the Church in the Old World would be abated in the New.

FOURTH LORD BALTIMORE

By injunction from abroad and by imitation in America the colonial governments imposed the pattern of animosity which had been revived in England. In some colonies, such as the Carolinas, no fresh legal invectives were incorporated into the statutes. The reason was that Catholics were few and certainly no attempt was made to hold services. Previously attention was called to Queen Anne having forced Pennsylvania to revise its laws so that they might include the proscriptions against Catholics. From the beginning of the 18th century, then, there was no place in the American colonies in which a Catholic was legally equal to his fellowmen.

Regardless of the locality, the imposition of stricter and increasingly severe regulations limited the growth of Catholic population. Even for those for whom it was possible, immigration to the New World offered no advantage in the practice of religion. Both in the mother country and in the colonies many weak Catholics undoubtedly lapsed from the Faith rather than suffer harsh penalties. Already lamentation has been uttered over the loss of Maryland as a Catholic refuge. A like reversal took place in the Calverts, who had labored so manfully to establish Maryland. On the death of his father in 1715 the fourth Lord Baltimore was confronted with the choice of losing his proprietorship in America or his Catholicity. He chose to apostatize. That he was termed "a degenerate scion of a noble Roman Catholic house" would have had little value had it not been written by the Protestant historian, Sanford H. Cobb.

To cite the penalties imposed in various colonies on Catholics and more especially on priests actually would be a distortion of history. This was an age accustomed to harshness. Minor civil infractions often were subject to dire punishment. For a sensitive or cultured person the social ostracism which accompanied his Catholicism inflicted wounds more difficult to bear than the lash. Catholic practices of no possible harm to others were first ridiculed and then banned by law. In Massachusetts Bay, for instance, the celebration of Christmas was forbidden because it was said to smack of "Popery." Nor was "guilt by association" unknown. As late as

1741 John Ury was hanged in New York on the suspicion that he was a priest. As far as can be determined the charge was without foundation, but nonetheless Ury suffered an ignominious death.

SURVIVAL A MYSTERY

Events far distant and over which absolutely no control could be exercised aroused dormant colonial anti-Catholicism. From the accession of William and Mary four wars were fought by England against Catholic nations, chiefly France and Spain. Not only were the colonies drawn into the struggles but the lurid flames of intolerance were rekindled. Ministers lashed at the Church from the pulpit; civil officials grasped the opportunity for fresh enactments against the faithful. Laws were passed for disarming "Papists," and it is easy to conceive the social odium which accompanied such summary action. Apparently even militant patriotism could not dispel the suspicion engendered by hatred of a misunderstood Faith. The records of Pennsylvania show that trader George Crogan had won the confidence of the Indians on the frontier. When war broke out he commanded his redskin friends under General Braddock. But his valor could not offset his known Catholicism! The governors of three provinces had him under surveillance solely because of his religion.

Thus belabored by clubs and impoverished by taxes, Catholics in the colonies managed to avert extermination until the middle of the 18th century. Their survival to that point still is a mystery. Even more severe attacks were to be endured before the American Revolution itself brought some toleration. From the Old Testament to these staunch upholders of the Faith may be transferred the tribute: "Giants were upon the earth in those days" (Gen. 6:4).

Chapter VI

THE QUEBEC ACT A CAUSE OF
THE AMERICAN REVOLUTION

EIGHTEENTH CENTURY AMERICAN CATHOLICS MAY HAVE THOUGHT that they had plumbed the nadir of colonial intolerance during the French and Indian War. The Acadians had felt the deepest bite of the lash in expulsion from their native Nova Scotia. Southward in the territory now the United States the "Act for disarming the Papists" must have been extremely humiliating for any Catholic of consequence. Whether or not an individual's house was searched for weapons, the suspicion cast upon his loyalty entirely because of his religion presented a severe test of his fidelity to the Church. In adopting the animosity of the government of the mother country toward the ancient religion, colonial anti-Catholicism had out-heroded Herod.

HOPES DASHED

The fall of Quebec not only brought death to the gallant Marshal Montcalm but also extinction of New France. In the Treaty of Paris of 1763 the French monarchy ceded all claim to the vast territory north and west of the British colonies. For Catholics living in the English provinces it must have brought a rosy gleam of

36

hope. No longer would any reason exist for charging the faithful with sympathy for their coreligionists fighting under the Lilies of France. Could they not look forward to a definite improvement in their status?

All these expectations were dashed in the controversy which arose both in England and in the colonies over the Quebec Act. The fresh difficulty for the Catholics in the English colonies originated in the refusal of the French and Spanish governments to jettison their former subjects at the peace conference. The defeated powers had insisted the all-conquering government of King George III not discriminate against the newly acquired inhabitants because of their Catholicity. This solicitude resulted in the inclusion of the following clause in the Treaty of Paris: "His Brittanic Majesty . . . agrees to grant the liberty of the Catholic religion to the inhabitants of Canada . . . . " Announced by proclamation on the Feast of the Most Holy Rosary of 1763, the Quebec Act was hotly debated on both sides of the Atlantic for 11 long years. Becoming a law on the eve of the American Revolution, it unquestionably was a cause of the colonial rebellion.

One instance will indicate that the Catholics in America did not presume upon the freedom proposed by the Quebec Act. With any priest subject to expulsion or even death if apprehended in the English colonies, it will be readily appreciated that no bishop was present. Once the territory east of the Mississippi was united under one rule, the Holy See proposed that Bishop Jean Olivier Briand of Quebec visit the faithful along the Atlantic seaboard, especially in Pennsylvania and Maryland.

Father Ferdinand Farmer's response to the suggestion was prompt and decisive. This zealous priest pointed out to Bishop Briand that any indulgence enjoyed was contrary to the letter of the law. The presence of a bishop, even temporarily, might invite summary action. This disaster would counterbalance by far the obvious benefits of the episcopal visit, even the spiritual advantages of the sacraments conferred.

"CATHOLICKS" EXCEPTED

Almost two hundred years later it would appear that the priest had correctly interpreted the ill temper of American non-Catholics of the 1770's. A review of the more flagrant incidents of these years will suffice. One had taken place the previous year. The Boston Committee of Correspondence had enumerated the causes of dissatisfaction among the settlers. One of the rights demanded was "to worship according to the dictates of one's own conscience." But while insisting upon this freedom from the mother country, the New Englanders explicitly denied it to "the Roman Catholicks." In addition to the usual vituperation of "Babylon's Whore," as the Church was branded, they cited the British Toleration Act of 1689 as a firm legal precedent for this disbarment.

No dissent was voiced to this exception in any of the 13 colonies. With an increase in the disagreement between parent and children, the famous Suffolk Resolves were passed by the New Englanders in 1774. Article 10 of these resolutions explicitly condemned the freedom of conscience granted to Roman Catholics in Canada as "dangerous in an extreme degree to the Protestant religion and to the civil rights and liberties of all Americans." Paul Revere carried a copy of the declaration to the Continental Congress. That body promptly approved without qualification all the resolutions and broadcast them to the newspapers throughout the colonies. More and more does it become clear that the Quebec Act was a direct cause of the American Revolution.

ANIMOSITY DEEP-SEATED

The ability of the men who comprised the First Continental Congress has been acknowledged both by those who favored the position of the colonies and those who supported the mother country. What was the attitude of men of this high caliber toward Catholicism? The written statements which this body composed and approved stand witness to the innermost sentiments of the members. Addresses were sent to the King, declarations issued of rights and grievances, and an appeal made to the people of Great Britain, all during the month of October, 1774. Every one of these declarations listed the Quebec Act as an injustice to the colonists and an intent to enslave them. The exact language of the affirmation to the people of Great Britain should be a reliable indicator of the detestation these gentlemen had toward Catholicism. Therein it was characterized as "a religion that has deluged your island with blood, and dispersed impiety, bigotry, persecution, murder and rebellion through every part of the world."

So it was no uneducated mob or a few demagogues who hurled the invectives against the Church in the English colonies. The tradition of animosity toward Catholics and their beliefs was so deep-seated that there were scarcely any who even questioned this antagonism.

Expediency and the realization that actual physical help might be needed accounts for the appeal to the Canadians, rather than lack of conviction by the Continental Congress in its fulminations against the Church.

The Address to the Inhabitants of Quebec was dispatched also in this month of October, 1774. The Quebec Act itself had been written for the benefit of these people, who had been subjects of the British crown for only slightly more than a decade. Catholicism being free and unrestricted had been the principal irritant in the Quebec Act to the English colonists. Yet the appeal for a united stand by them against the mother country included this statement: "We are all too well acquainted with the liberality of sentiment distinguishing your nation, to imagine that differences of religion would prejudice you against a hearty amity with us." Is it possible to conceive a more complete reversal of position than was displayed by the First Continental Congress within a few days? More truly may it be asserted that no change in sentiment had occurred. With almost the same pen as had written the appeal to the Canadians there was dispatched a second *Petition to the King.* Therein the members of the Congress repeated their complaint about the freedom extended Catholics in the North!

CATHOLICS COURAGEOUS

War clouds are always foreboding; but come war or peace, the colonial Catholics of 1775 apparently had no hope of an improved situation. True, Great Britain had abated her anti-Catholic measures for the benefit of the Canadians. The virulence of the protest provoked negated any expectation of the indulgence being broadened to include "these free Protestant colonies." On the other hand, those promoting a complete breach of the ties with the mother country were the very ones most bitter in vilifying the Church. Retention of their heritage of Faith in the face of increasing oppression had long since proved the courage and fortitude of the colonial Catholics. The enthusiasm with which this beleaguered group joined the struggle for national as well as religious liberty will be inspiring to every American today.

Chapter VII

THE LIBERTY BELL RINGS OUT
FOR AMERICAN CATHOLICS

THAT GOD CAN AND DOES DRAW GOOD OUT OF EVIL IS PROVED
over and over again. A striking instance of this Divine Providence
is found in the Quebec Act of 1774. Initially it seemed that this
legislation, in permitting Catholicity to be freely professed and
practiced by Canadians, would cause laws against the Church in
the 13 colonies to become even more coercive. Instead it afforded
the Catholics in the colonies an opportunity for the first time to
demonstrate their loyalty as a group. To this day the Church in the
United States benefits from the valor of the Catholics of '76.

As the breach between mother country and colonies widened,
it was apparent to every leader of the patriots that all the help
available would be needed. Historians agree that only one-third of
the colonists resisted Great Britain, then the strongest military
power of the world. For any who were willing to shoulder a mus-
ket, in the words of St. Paul, "There is neither Jew nor Greek;
there is neither slave nor freeman; there is neither male nor female"
(Gal. 3:28). In the English colonies for the first time it could be
said that Catholics were truly welcomed.

On two occasions Catholic efforts to assist the American Revolution were hampered by the prior colonial anti-Catholicism. The

Indians of Maine, long since converted to the Faith, volunteered on condition that General Washington provide them with a chaplain. The commander-in-chief referred the request to Massachusetts, of which Maine was then a part. Laws more than a century old prohibiting the presence of a priest in the colony showed their effect. Not only was the colonial government not able to call upon a priest in that vast territory, but no idea was had where one might be found. Finally the request of the Indians was fulfilled through an exchange of prisoners for a priest who had been a chaplain aboard a French ship taken as a prize of war.

Farther to the north was another disappointment which was of much greater consequence. After berating King George III for the freedom granted to the Catholics of Canada, the First Continental Congress had besought these same Canadians to join their cause. When war actually broke out a commission was chosen to plead in person. Anti-Catholicism had kept Maryland's "First Citizen," Charles Carroll of Carrollton, from participating in the assembly. But he was readily named as one of the three members of the delegation to appeal for aid from the French Catholics to the north. The same Continental Congress asked Father John Carroll, cousin of Charles, to accompany the mission. From letters to his mother it is evident that Father Carroll had little hope of success. Yet he willingly did his best to convince the Canadians that the previous diatribes against the Church did not represent the true American spirit. Bishop Jean Olivier Briand, however, was so grateful for the freedom already bestowed by the British government that he kept Canada loyal to the Crown.

Charles Carroll was due to exert still more influence for the patriot cause, and this time most effectively. The colonial leaders were ready to make a complete break with the mother country. One of the signers of the Declaration of Independence was Charles Carroll, who brought honor to the Church in being the sole Catholic. Moreover, he had another distinction which was convincing proof of his patriotism. The richest man in the colonies, Carroll risked that fortune as well as his life in proclaiming openly his full adherence to the Revolution. To his clearly legible signature he added "of Carrollton." It is said that his purpose in so doing was that there would be no mistake as to his identity should the revolt fail and the signers be punished. Fifty-three years later Carroll, then the only surviving signer of the Declaration of Independence, told the adopted son of George Washington that the love of his religion as well as of his country had prompted his action. Referring to the freedom to practice his Faith he said of his signing: "I had much at heart this grand design founded on mutual charity, the basis of our holy religion." His courageous venture paid immediate dividends to the forces led by George Washington, for the Catholics of Pennsylvania and Maryland followed his example in their whole-hearted support.

The valor of the patriots and the leadership of Washington would not have been successful had foreign aid not been secured. It was to Catholic France that the first appeal was made. In the beginning a few leaders protested dealing with "Foreign Papists," but the danger from the British forces was too imminent for them to be heeded. Supplies absolutely essential had been sent by France long before the Treaty of Alliance was signed in May of 1778. Congress was elated! To the credit of that body it showed its gratitude consistently throughout the war. Occasionally individual members demurred, but as a group the Congress divested itself entirely of anti-Catholic expressions of any kind. Elbridge Gerry of Massachusetts did marvel at the "miraculous change in the political world." If not strictly miraculous, the effects of this alliance — with later aid from Catholic Spain — truly were monumental in history.

It is not surprising that the Tories — one-third of the Americans who supported England in the struggle — took horrified umbrage at the alliance of the colonies with "Papist France." In their eyes the specter of the Pope was seen hovering above every French soldier. All previous canards seemingly were refuted in the exemplary conduct of the French troops who passed through Philadelphia in 1781. Nonetheless, one loyalist writer construed the good behavior as absolute proof that the "French Papists" were awaiting a more suitable time to disclose the cloven hoof.

Help from Spain was not of the same magnitude as that of her sister Bourbon power France, but again the American Congress broke completely with tradition in showing appreciation. Not the words of a friend but those of a bitter enemy describe the action after the 1778 death of the Spanish representative in Philadelphia, Don Juan de Miralles. The most infamous of all American traitors, Benedict Arnold, wrote: "Do you know that the eye which guides this pen lately saw your mean and profligate Congress at Mass for the soul of a Roman Catholic in Purgatory?" The Solemn Requiem had been celebrated in St. Mary's Church in Philadelphia.

The patriot newspapers of the colonies were as consistent in supporting the alliance with France as was Congress. Formerly loud in their denunciation of anything which had even a Catholic flavor, the newspapers then became positively enthusiastic in their reports pertaining to our ally. Equally noteworthy was the complete acceptance of the military union by the Calvinist clergy. Once the King of France had rivaled the Pope as an object of denunciation. That attitude had been completely abandoned when the Reverend George Duffield, from the pulpit of the Third Presbyterian Church of Philadelphia, called for an end to detraction; inherited prejudices should give way to cordial affection.

There is surprisingly little to quote from Catholics in praise or in endorsement of the league with France. In 1777 the French Consul at Baltimore observed that the Maryland Catholics "feared an alliance with France, lest they be persecuted, and lest their priests be expelled." The rack and rope of anti-Catholicism were retained in the minds of the faithful long after others had renounced these instruments of torture.

To the outcome of the struggle Longfellow's words may be applied: "You know the rest. In the books you have read . . . " God indeed had drawn good out of evil for the long-suffering Catholics of 18th-century America. While the tradition of anti-Catholicism had not been shattered, undoubtedly its previously unbroken front had been penetrated. The American Revolution brought liberty to the colonies; moreover it brought to the American Catholics a real hope of freedom of conscience. For most of them the shackles would not vanish immediately or completely. But never again would the outlook be as bleak, nor the very survival of Catholicism in America be threatened.

Chapter VIII

FEDERAL RELIGIOUS EQUALITY NOT REALIZED IN ALL THE STATES

As long as there is a United States of America Catholics will be proud of the glorious part taken by their forefathers in the American Revolution. During the Colonial period anti-Catholicism had kept their numbers so small as to be almost insignificant. Yet in the struggle Catholics contributed a part all out of proportion to their percentage of the total population. Martin I. J. Griffin of Philadelphia has contended, moreover, that no Catholic of note was a loyalist, or a supporter of Great Britain. Truly the record is remarkable!

INDIVIDUAL LAWS

What was the reaction of the non-Catholic majority, most of them churchgoers, to this impressive Catholic participation? When the Revolution began Catholics did not possess religious, social, or political equality in a single one of the colonies. Among the courageous signers of the Declaration of Independence Charles Carroll of Carrollton had been the sole Catholic. Years later the venerable Marylander had declared that he had envisioned religious liberty as well as political freedom from the successful defense of this document. Indeed Carroll was right, but the actual attainment of it was to be delayed — in some cases for many, many years. Why?

It must be remembered that the War of the Revolution was fought by a very loose political union. All the erstwhile colonies were represented in the Continental Congress. That body, however, had no power to enforce its wishes, and as a unit it expressed none regarding religious freedom for all. Each of the seceding colonies operated under its own individual laws. Inasmuch as all of these had contained anti-Catholic provisions prior to the outbreak of the fighting, the legal position of Catholics would remain unaffected unless the charters or constitutions were altered.

Some, as Connecticut, were content with the original colonial charter; aside from erasing a few English names, no change was made. South Carolina, on the other hand, promptly adopted a new constitution which contained no provision regarding religion. In 1778, the year that Catholic France gave its invaluable assistance to the Americans, a revised constitution made Protestantism the religion of South Carolina. In addition, anyone not a Protestant was ineligible for the upper or lower house of the legislature. In New York the incongruity of fighting for liberty and denying it to some was recognized in the Constitutional Convention. But John Jay, later the first Chief Justice of the United States, was an inveterate foe of Catholicism. Failing to block the article granting religious freedom, he succeeded in securing an amendment which deprived immigrant Catholics of any participation in the political life of the new state.

"NOMINAL" EMANCIPATION

Previously it has been noted that the majority of Catholics were living in the area close to the boundary lines of Maryland, Pennsylvania, and Delaware. The constitutions of these states reflected their presence in not excluding the faithful from the provisions for religious liberty. The few Catholics in northern Virginia profited from the challenge by Baptists and Presbyterians to Anglicanism as the established religion. The controversy was not settled during the Revolution; yet Catholics benefited when full religious freedom was adopted by Virginia in 1785. Two years before Rhode Island had dropped "except Papists" from her guarantee of religious equality.

While the military and financial aid of Catholics was everywhere welcome, only four states had given them the right to vote. Even in Maryland, in the opinion of the Reverend Jonathan Boucher, a prominent loyalist minister from that state, "their emancipation . . . has been nominal rather than real."

Hanging the Pope in effigy had been banned by George Washington at the very beginning of the Revolution. Once the struggle had been successful, however, such carnivals were revived in New England and continued for another century. In his 1785 participation in a lecture series given annually in Cambridge, the Reverend Joseph Willard, Congregationalist President of Harvard University, declared that the spirit of the Church of Rome was "hatred, malice, and persecution." By no means had the Revolution overturned the persistent anti-Catholic tradition throughout the 13 states.

Originally proposed by Benjamin Franklin in 1755, national union may be said to have come into existence with the adoption of the Articles of Confederation in 1778. Maryland was the last state to give her adherence to this confederacy of the former colonies. Again it was a Carroll, in this instance Charles' cousin Daniel, who was the sole Catholic signer. While the Constitutional Convention was in session the government under the Articles of Confederation issued the renowned Northwest Ordinance. Therein for the first time in the history of our nation the principle of religious freedom for all was enunciated for states to be formed from this territory.

EMERGENCE FROM "CATACOMBS"

A little over a month later the Constitutional Convention adopted a resolution which had been proposed by Charles Pinckney of South Carolina; this resolution is in Article Six of the Constitution. It read "No religious test shall ever be required as a qualification to any office or public trust under the United States." The only state voting against Pinckney's resolution was North Carolina. That was in keeping with the tenor of the state's Constitutional Convention. The Mecklenburg delegates, for instance, were instructed to oppose "the toleration of popish idolatrous worship." Nonetheless, while still excluded from most state and local offices, Catholics were recognized as first-class citizens on the national level! In place of the one signer of the Declaration of Independence and of the Articles of Confederation, there were two representatives of the Faith among the Founding Fathers of the Constitution. One was Daniel Carroll, and the second an Irish immigrant who had helped to finance the Revolution, Thomas FitzSimons of Pennsylvania.

While the anti-Catholic tradition was being shivered if not shattered, the Church began to emerge from its American catacombs. Though some authority definitely was needed, the clergy still opposed the naming of a bishop lest that arouse renewed antagonism. As a compromise Father John Carroll was named Prefect Apostolic in 1784. In his initial report to the Holy See he estimated 25,000 as the Catholic population of the United States. He had heard that there were Catholics along the Mississippi River, where in truth the "Patriot Priest" Pierre Gibault had been of sterling assistance to George Rogers Clark in the conquest of the West. With the help of a thousand dollars from King Charles III of Spain, the first church in New York was dedicated in 1786.

But there was not a single Catholic church or congregation in all New England nor in any state south of Virginia.

THE FIRST BISHOP

The United States was a small nation in population the year that George Washington was inaugurated as the first President. Catholics composed an almost insignificant group in the total of 4,000,000. Yet among them were men of national stature and prominence, so that a letter of congratulations to the President was graciously acknowledged. The Father of His Country wrote in part:

> I presume that your fellow citizens will not forget the patriotic part which you took in the accomplishment of their Revolution, and the establishment of your Government: or the important assistance which they received from a nation in which the Roman Catholic Faith is professed.

How greatly had the position of the Church improved over what it had been a century before! It was vastly better than during the furor over the Quebec Act. Many outside the Church retained their old prejudices, but a substantial number had come to accept Catholic fellow Americans in all social relations. Legal disabilities remained for the most part. Inspiration and leadership in triumphing over many of these obstacles was to come from John Carroll. Consecrated the first bishop of the United States in 1790, he was a worthy contemporary of George Washington. As truly as Washington was the father of his country, the first Bishop and Archbishop of Baltimore was the father of the Church in the United States.

Chapter IX

CATHOLIC NEWSPAPERS ESTABLISHED TO COMBAT PRINTED ABUSE

IN THE EARLY YEARS OF THE 19TH CENTURY A CATHOLIC COULD have viewed life in these United States with great satisfaction. The number of the faithful had grown steadily, with natural increase and conversions aided slightly by immigrants from the Old World.

The first bishop of the Church in the United States, John Carroll, had the respect of all who knew him. In 1808 he became the first archbishop of the country, with four new dioceses coming into being at the same time. The spirit John Cotton had expressed in saying that "it was toleration that made the world anti-Christian" 150 years before in Massachusetts Bay Colony apparently was fast waning.

SEAL OF CONFESSIONAL CHALLENGED

In many places today expressways and toll roads are provided to allow transportation accelerated above that of ordinary streets and highways. The United States of Jefferson's administration would be intolerable in this respect, for even the large cities were hardly connected with a passable road. Likewise, modern Americans would be appalled at the onerous restrictions against Catholics which some states then retained. In general, however, the

51

magnanimity expressed by the Founding Fathers in the Constitution had been infectious. Sometimes through a single individual a whole state benefited. The Test Oath was rescinded in New York, for instance, because the competence of Catholic Francis Cooper prompted his fellow citizens to remove the prohibition on a Catholic holding public office. Perhaps the "Land of the Free" might soon be realized on the state level as well as in the guarantees of the Federal Constitution.

Occasionally the improvement in the position of the faithful prompted a reaction by those who were incensed at any recognition of the "Church of Rome." During the War of 1812 stolen property was returned by a New York resident who was a penitent of Father Anthony Kohlmann. When the priest refused to testify in court the cry went up that the confessional was a shield for thieves, and Father Kohlmann was indicted. The court demanding he answer, the priest replied: "It would be my duty to prefer instantaneous death or any temporal misfortune, rather than disclose the name of the penitent in question." While all the judges were Protestants, speaking through DeWitt Clinton the New York tribunal ruled the priest could not be forced to testify.

This legal recognition of the seal of the confessional roiled some who were intensely anti-Catholic. A series of pamphlets and writings spewed forth, flaying the Church and her members. No doubt saner heads would have prevailed and the vituperation gradually subsided had not a new weight been added which temporarily unbalanced the scales of traditional American justice.

Europe had been involved in war almost from the time of the American Revolution. The United States had been drawn into the struggle in 1812. After peace came in 1815 there was an upsurge in immigration to the United States. Though it was a trickle compared with the torrent of mid-century and thereafter, the influx of people inevitably incited hostility. Some were unable to see the need for additional labor for the new factories, for opening the West, and for internal improvements, such as national roads. Most of the newcomers were poor and few were educated. Yet Professor Ray Allen Billington holds that these and other objections were minor. "Fundamentally," he has emphasized, "the aliens were opposed because they were Catholics. . . ." Hostility did not become inordinate and widespread at once, but the rancor grew as steadily as an untreated ulcer.

BISHOP ENGLAND

Notwithstanding, during these years it appeared that an improved understanding was being reached between American Catholics and those not of the Faith. Several positive advances came from Irish-born John England, first Bishop of Charleston. Mass had not been offered in South Carolina until 1786, and then by a priest from a ship which had halted in Charleston's harbor. It was from this same "Palmetto State" that the first Catholic newspaper, *The United States Catholic Miscellany,* was commenced by Bishop England two years after his arrival. Never of large circulation, the journal nevertheless was distributed throughout the country. It continued to present Catholic teaching from 1822 until it was added to the casualties of the War between the States.

In addition to the newspaper, Bishop England used the spoken word to make the Church better known. Recognition of his eloquence and sincerity came in an invitation to address the United States Congress. On January 8, 1826, President John Quincy Adams, the Senate, and the House of Representatives listened to the bishop for two and one half hours. With his gifted tongue Bishop England explained Catholic doctrine to this assemblage of distinguished Protestants. Only in concluding did he refer to the increasing tension and then it was to plead that "our harmony and union here below may produce that peace and good will that may be emblematic of our enjoyment of more lasting happiness in a better world."

Partly to answer the taunts and calumnies which had commenced with the judicial upholding of the seal of the confessional, publication of the *Truth Teller* was initiated in New York in 1825. In the next few years more and more bishops followed the example of John England in using newspapers to answer critics of the Church. How these adversaries did multiply! In addition to the irritant of immigration two other happenings engendered opposition and even hatred of the Church.

ANTI-CATHOLIC LITERATURE

One was from the first font of anti-Catholicism in America, England. The rigor of many penal laws was relaxed or removed by Parliament's passage of the 1829 Catholic Emancipation Act. By no means was this belated justice unopposed in the British Isles. Hundreds of pamphlets were printed in England and made their way to the United States. These vilifications of the Church were distributed here; with the ancient libels retained they were oftentimes reprinted without reference to the Emancipation Act. Over and above the pamphlets were about 30 newspapers whose sole or principal topic was the "Church of Rome." Most infamous among them was *The Protestant,* started in New York in the first month of 1830. The initial article commented on the revival of the Jesuits. It continued: "The sleepless and wily exertions of the devotees of 'The Man of Sin' [appellation leveled at the Pope] constitute a serious topic of scrutiny to all persons. . . . It is therefore intended to issue a weekly paper which shall be exclusively devoted to a portraiture of Popery."

The previous year the first council or official meeting of the bishops of the United States was held in Baltimore. This convocation had been urged in order to counteract this simmering cauldron of abuse. An official concilar letter to the laity pleaded for charity and affection among the adherents of all denominations.

This sentence was worthy of pondering by all: "To God and not to you, nor to us, do they stand or fail; to Him and not to us is reserved the judgment of individuals." In the opinion of the same Northwestern University Professor Billington the exhortation was vain. He believed that this council of bishops stimulated anti-Catholicism in the national attention it called to the growth and progress of the Catholic Church.

"CATHOLIC PRESS"

Catholics were still sparse in New England when a journal to present the Faith rightly was first published in 1829. Most of the enthusiasm and the financing came from the convert-family of the Taylors of Connecticut. The first issue prompted a Protestant organ of Hartford to publish a caustic editorial on "Romanism in Connecticut" which ended with the query: "How would it read in history that in 1829, Hartford, in the State of Connecticut, was made the center of a Roman Catholic Mission?"

In an unruffled manner the *Catholic Press* ventured "it would read exceedingly well."

The second Bishop of Boston was a Jesuit, Benedict Joseph Fenwick. On his first visitation to Maine he found Catholics at Belfast afraid to confess their religion because of fear of their neighbors. Impelled to strengthen these faithful as well as to counteract the assaults, in the same year, 1829, Bishop Fenwick founded in Boston a Catholic journal. Its antecedents are indicated in the title, *The Jesuit,* which was not so happy a name for restraining hostile pens and voices. This paper was a predecessor of the Boston *Pilot* of today. An 1832 quotation from the hostile Rochester *Observer* will demonstrate the need for enlightenment about the true teachings of the Church. It read:

A person who is condemned to purgatory for 5,000,-000,000 years can have the time shortened, and the sufferings diminished, by procuring the Pope's order upon the devil, who is the jailor; and so intimate are these two mighty potentates, that it is affirmed Satan never yet refused his friend's draft and order for the release of a soul favored by the Pope.

CANDLES IN THE DARKNESS

It was through these Taylors of Connecticut that a Catholic publication began in far distant St. Louis. In 1832, when Deodat Taylor offered to undertake the venture Bishop Joseph Rosati wrote in his diary: "I will assist him with all my power." At the moment the bishop could have given no financial aid, but soon Pope Gregory XVI sent him $3,000 to help complete the cathedral commenced the previous year. From this money Bishop Rosati diverted two hundred dollars to establish the newspaper *Shepherd of the Valley*. The magnitude of the bishop's appropriation can be better understood when it is noted that the Easter collection that year in the cathedral parish was $150.00.

The lowering clouds of anti-Catholicism were not to be dispersed until a terrific storm had been endured. If the attack was not repelled, the defenders of the Faith undoubtedly were strengthened by the dozen Catholic newspapers commenced during these years. With Jesus Christ the Light of the World, these journals may be regarded as 12 candles burning in the darkness. All the blackness was not dispelled, but the little flames betokened the determined survival of the Faith.

Chapter **X**

INFLAMMATORY DIATRIBES IGNITE CHARLESTOWN CONVENT

THE INAUGURATION OF ANDREW JACKSON AS PRESIDENT OF THE United States in 1829 brought a throng of his friends to Washington from their homes beyond the Alleghenies. Nationalism and Americanism were no mere academic ideas but woven into the fabric of this administration. To that extent it could be said to have been unfriendly to the strengthening tide of immigrants, and many newcomers to our shores were inevitably linked with Catholicism. Agitators labeled even those incomers who declared themselves Protestants as "Jesuits in disguise."

FIRST CATHOLIC CABINET MEMBER

Except in this general sense of some exaggeration of Americanism Jackson's administration was not antagonistic to the Church. In fact, the hero of the Battle of New Orleans named the first Catholic member of a presidential cabinet in the person of Roger Brooke Taney. The numerous newspapers whose business was anti-Catholicism raged at the choice of this Maryland-born jurist for Attorney-General. The ranting was as ineffectual against the President's determination as the whisperings of the Washington matrons against Peggy Eaton. Taney went on to be elevated to the bench of the Supreme Court. Rejected once by the United States Senate, he was confirmed in 1836 as the first Catholic Chief Justice. Needless to say, the wild predictions that the Pope would soon follow Taney to Washington were not fulfilled during the 28 long years the Marylander presided over the nation's supreme tribunal.

Both numerically and proportionately Catholics were increasing in the United States in these 1830's, though the total was still not much more than one half million. But it would have seemed that there were far more than one Catholic out of every 25 Americans from the abuse directed against the faithful. While backstairs gossip or pulpit harangues cannot be heard today, much of the anti-Catholic literature may still be read. Pamphlets written in England against the Catholic Emancipation Act of 1829 were circulated on this side of the Atlantic Ocean. Indicative of the financial profit possible, as well as the deepness of the animosity, was the appearance of numerous books.

The inventor Samuel F. B. Morse frequently dipped his pen in vitriol against the Church. Probably not the cause at all, but the immediate occasion for his hatred had been his experience while visiting Rome. When he had not removed his hat while watching a Church procession, a soldier had knocked off his indecorous chapeau. It is not known if Morse's hat was damaged but his dignity certainly was offended. For years the Church in the United States suffered from the abuse heaped upon her because one soldier in Rome decided for himself to force a respectful demeanor from an unbelieving visitor.

In 1790 George Washington had told his Catholic countrymen that "as mankind becomes more liberal they will be more apt to allow that all who conduct themselves as worthy members of the community are equally entitled to the protection of civil government." The first President's optimism was far from realization in the Massachusetts of 1834. At Charlestown, to which Paul Revere had rowed from Boston, the Ursuline nuns had established Mount St. Benedict, a school for young ladies. Those of the Catholics who were recent immigrants had little money to spend on higher education for their daughters. But with four-fifths of the students non-Catholics the institution expanded. The nuns scrupulously adhered to their promise not to impose their own religious convictions on those not of the Faith.

"BRIMSTONE CORNER"

As the academy prospered and grew, bitter remarks were directed against it by enemies of the Church. Many non-Catholic ministers were particularly incensed that wealthy Unitarians of the Boston area patronized the school. Leader of the attacks was the Reverend Lyman Beecher, pastor of Boston's Park Street Church. His fiery castigations of Catholicism from that pulpit earned for it the popular designation of "Brimstone Corner."

Two unfortunate incidents caused the bubbling cauldron to boil over. A scullery maid who had asked to be admitted to the Ursuline order was dismissed as unsuitable after four months. A lurid account of convent life was issued under her name, but probably would have been dismissed by all save the overly credulous had not an actual nun left the convent school. This overworked music teacher temporarily lost her reason and fled to the home of friends. When she had recovered her senses the following day she was visited by Bishop Benedict Joseph Fenwick, for whom she had sent. He readily granted permission for her to return to the convent and she was brought back by her Protestant brother. Rumors of the incident were magnified by hostile elements and within a week were flaunted in two Boston newspapers. At first it was intimated she had been cast into a dungeon; then it was charged that she could not be found at the convent at all. Sunday evening,

August 10, the Reverend Lyman Beecher called for action against "Popery" in violent sermons delivered in three separate Boston churches. While some Catholic writers have charged that these onslaughts were responsible for the devastation which followed, it is probable that the wealthy congregations addressed by Beecher did not actually participate in the foray. There is evidence which apparently indicates that lower elements of the area's population had planned attacking the convent for some time before the nun had suffered her nervous breakdown.

TARDY REFUTATION

A short time before, Bishop Fenwick had had a difference with the selectmen of Charlestown over a Catholic cemetery. "For health reasons" the councilmen had refused to grant a permit, though non-Catholics were being buried in the same area without any apparent contamination of air or earth. This may have accounted for tardy action on the part of the councilmen. However, on Monday morning, August 11, five selectmen made a tour of the convent and talked with the nun who had left temporarily. They issued a statement to the Boston newspapers that nothing objectionable had been found, and that the young lady in question "expresses herself to be entirely satisfied with the present situation, it being that of her own choice."

Alas! This complete refutation of all charges was one day too late. When it was printed the convent already had been attacked and burned to the ground. In their nightdress the nuns, together with the children and young ladies in their charge, escaped through a rear gate of the surrounding garden. "Not content with all this," an investigating committee of non-Catholics reported, "they burst open the tomb of the establishment, and exposed to view the mouldering remains of their tenants. . . . Not one arm was lifted in the defense of helpless women and children."

The next day a mass meeting of Protestants was held in Faneuil Hall under the leadership of Boston's Mayor Theodore Lyman, Jr. The destruction of the convent was denounced as a "base and cowardly act." Meanwhile from nearby railroad construction camps Irish laborers had started on a mission of revenge. When he heard of this Bishop Fenwick hurried six priests in different directions to stay the self-appointed vigilantes. Calling Boston Catholics together, he urged his listeners to remain quiet and allow the law to take its course. The Boston *Gazette* commented: "We hope the bishop will furnish us with a copy of his address for publication. It would be read with a high degree of satisfaction by his Protestant fellow citizens."

NO REDRESS

The trust of the bishop in legal vindication was not fulfilled. Of the mob which participated in the burning, eight were charged with arson. Authorities agree today that the trials were decided before the evidence was heard. All were acquitted save one youngster. He, too, was released on the petition of Boston Catholics, who refused to allow the youth to be scapegoat for those who had planned and carried out the felonious assault.

When Bishop Fenwick petitioned for funds to rebuild the convent, the matter was referred to the state legislature. The deep-seated hatred of the assailants was mirrored in this quotation from the *American Protestant Vindicator* of January, 1835:

> Any man who proposes, or would vote for the measure, which would rob the treasury of the descendants of the Puritans to build Ursuline nunneries . . . must be a raving lunatic.

The legislature rejected this and all subsequent attempts to give the Ursulines money to rebuild on the blackened foundation of their school. As late as 1854 Benjamin F. Butler of Civil War fame proposed compensation to the nuns, and his committee in the Massachusetts House enthusiastically approved. Once more anti-Catholic pressure was exerted; for the last time the attempt to indemnify the Ursulines was defeated.

ASSAULTS INCREASE

The immediate reaction of fair-minded Americans was astonishment and horror at the convent burning. In Boston a group headed by Harrison Gray Otis called on "all good citizens to express individually and collectively the abhorrence they feel of this high-handed violation of the laws." Even several religious papers which had been denouncing Mount St. Benedict were sympathetic to the Ursulines and repentant of the invectives which they had printed. Once released from the bounds of law and conscience, however, the mob spirit is difficult to control. Despite the protestations of influential Protestants, episodes similar in character were much too frequent in the succeeding months and years. Assaults on churches became so common in New England that Catholic parishioners took turns at patrolling the property. The danger was indicated by the refusal of some insurance companies to issue policies on Catholic buildings.

Hopeful omens were indeed difficult to discern in the period following the burning of Mount St. Benedict Convent. When the bishops assembled again in Baltimore in 1837 they approved a pastoral letter written by Bishop John England in which the Charlestown outrage was forcibly denounced. Notwithstanding, the pen of the South Carolina bishop wrote confidently of Catholic belief in and reliance on the freedom proclaimed in our national Constitution. "Bloody but unbowed" would be a pungent description of the Catholic in America in the late 1830's.

Chapter XI

ARCHBISHOP HUGHES' COURAGE HALTS ANTI-CATHOLIC RIOTS

PRODUCTION OF GASOLINE IN THE UNITED STATES HAD TO AWAIT the drilling of the first successful oil well in 1859 at Titusville, Pennsylvania. It would seem that some had been made in advance from the flash-fires of anti-Catholicism which flared in 1835 after the burning of Massachusetts' Ursuline convent. Once the stopper has been jerked from the jug of mob-violence, the insidious fumes are almost impossible to control. Remonstrances and appeals go unheeded because the action had even its beginning outside of the law.

Concerted action against the Church, however, awaited the formation of the Native American Party, which is believed to have begun at Germantown, Pennsylvania, in 1837. Its declaration of principles demanded that all public offices should be limited to native Americans only. The real objective of the party in attacking *Catholic* immigrants may be readily recognized from the epithets used in their newspapers: "Irish Papists," and the "degraded slaves of the Pope."

CHURCH BURNING

By 1844 the nativist party was known as the American Republican Association. Early in May Philadelphia members were notified to meet in the suburb of Kensington, heavily peopled with Irish. Under such provocation, of course, trouble broke out. Several were killed, scores injured, and 25 to 30 homes of Catholics were reduced to ashes. Though military aid was called, the next day two Catholic churches were burned to the ground. George Washington had contributed to the building of one of them, St. Augustine's. A school of the Sisters of Charity was likewise destroyed by flames. Almost exactly 11 years before, the Board of Guardians of Philadelphia had framed a resolution of thanks to other Sisters. The bravery and goodness they had shown in caring for cholera victims, the resolution declared, "entitled them to the warmest thanks and gratitude of the whole community, which has benefited by their labors." Now the appreciation had been shown by burning a Sisters' school to the ground.

The following Monday *The Spirit of the Times,* a secular newspaper of Philadelphia, commented on the large number of people who had gone to church the previous day to thank God for having been preserved from harm during the riots. "Into all churches, we should have said, excepting the Roman Catholic. . . . In obedience to the orders of the Bishop they were not opened for public worship." Bishop Francis Patrick Kenrick had sought sanctuary in the home of a Protestant friend. Notwithstanding, during the riots he had issued the following bulletin to the Catholics of his diocese:

> I earnestly conjure you all to avoid all occasion of excitement, and to shun all public places of assemblage, and to do nothing that in any way may exasperate. Follow peace with all men, and have that Charity without which no man can see God.

Not only were level-minded Philadelphians of every creed shocked by this debacle; the entire nation was horrified. The *Baptist Advocate* commented: "The will of the people is indis-

THE CATHOLIC
IN AMERICA

From Colonial Times to the
Present Day

by

Peter J. Rahill, Ph.D.

FRANCISCAN HERALD PRESS
Publishers of Franciscan Literature
Chicago 9, Illinois

18th CENTURY

1. The Acadians, expelled by the British from their homes in 1755, were refused admission to the Thirteen Colonies because they were Catholics.

THE
BOOK
OF
RATES,
Now used in the
Sin Custom-house
Of the CHURCH and COURT of
ROME.
CONTAINING
The BULLS, DISPENSATIONS, & PARDONS
for all manner of Villanies, and Wickednesse, with the
several sums of Monies given and to be paid for them.

PUBLISHED
By Anthony Egane; B. D. late Confessor-General of the
Kingdome of IRELAND, and now through the mercy of
God Minister of the Gospel according to the Reformed Religion.

Ephes. 5. 12. For it is a shame even to speak of those things which
are done of them in secret.

Licenced according to Order.

LONDON
Printed for Benjamin Southwood, at the Sign of the Star next to
Serjeants-Inn, in Chancery Lane, 1674.

A
DISCOURSE
ON THE
MAN OF SIN;
DELIVERED IN THE
CHAPEL OF HARVARD COLLEGE,
IN
CAMBRIDGE, NEW-ENGLAND,
SEPTEMBER 1, 1773:
AT THE LECTURE, FOUNDED
BY THE HONORABLE
PAUL DUDLEY, ESQ.
By SAMUEL COOPER, D.D.
Pastor of the Church in Brattle-Street, BOSTON.

BOSTON: Printed and Sold at GREENLEAF's
Printing-Office, in HANOVER-STREET,
M,DCC,LXXIV.

2. *The Book of Rates* is typical of anti-Catholic popular literature published in England during the 17th century.

3. "The Man of Sin" was an epithet applied to the Pope by anti-Catholic lecturers and writers.

5. The *Ark* and *Dove,* ships which carried the initial colonists to Maryland in 1634.

4. George Calvert, the first Lord Baltimore, to whom was granted the land on which the Catholic colony of Maryland was founded.

6. William Penn, Quaker founder of Pennsylvania, sought to protect Catholic settlers from English penal laws.

No person within the said colony, at any time hereafter, shall be any wise molested, punished, disquieted, or called in question for any differences of opinion in matters of religion, Roman Catholics alone excepted

—Statutes of Rhode Island, 1719

7. Excerpt of Statutes of Rhode Island, 1719.

8. Thomas Dongan, Catholic Governor of the Province of New York, 1682-1688.

9. "The First Prayer in Congress, 1774."

10. Father John Carroll, who pleaded the colonial cause in Canada in 1776, in this picture was the first Archbishop of Baltimore.

11. Charles Carroll of Carrollton, American Revolutionary leader and sole Catholic signer of the Declaration of Independence.

12. Daniel Carroll, American patriot and one of the two Catholic signers of the Constitution of the United States.

3. John Jay, American patriot and urist, persisted in his unfriendliess to Catholics.

THE CATHOLIC INVASION

frequent in those days than these, and beside the anti-Roman hell-fire of the *Vindicators* the *Fellowship Forums* and *Rail Splitters* of our day pale into insignificance.

In 1830 a number of ministers of the Presbyterian and Dutch Reformed Churches launched a newspaper called the *Protestant*, with seventy-two ministers as patrons, under the direction of Dr. Brownlee,[1] who publicly and privately advertised the paper and urged its promotion. The following are a few extracts showing the violent and scurrilous character of this sheet:

PROGRESS OF POPERY

Jersey, Elizabethtown.—On the 13th of September 103 persons were confirmed in their idolatry; and the Mass-house is about to be very much enlarged.

Clearfield.—A new temple for the Mass was opened on October 4th and twenty-five persons entered themselves as vassals of Babylon the Great.

Huntingdon.—On the 7th of October fifty-two persons received the mark of the beast.

Ebbenburg.—On October 14th and the next day 120 persons received the seal of the man of sin and the graveyard was sprinkled with Roman salt water.

Pittsburg, Pa.—On November 7th a female proselyte and seven other persons became practitioners in the mysterious iniquity of the Convent.

In 1831 took place the famous debate between Father John Hughes, afterward Archbishop of New York, and the Rev. John Breckenridge, a Presbyterian minister of high standing. The controversy was waged in the pages of the *Presbyterian* and the *Catholic Herald*. It was marked by great bitterness and many personalities. Religious papers of all denominations indulged in extreme and ill-grounded statements which would not be permitted today. The Second Provincial Council of Baltimore which met about

[1] Dr. W. C. Brownlee was a minister of the Dutch Reformed Church in New York City, a man of violent temper and unrelenting in his hostility to the Catholic Church. He was connected with practically every anti-Catholic activity of his day.

63

14. "Progress of Popery," extracts from the *Protestant,* an 1830 New York newspaper.

He saith to him again: Simon son of John, lovest thou me? He saith to him: Yea Lord, thou knowest that I love thee. He saith to him: Feed my lambs.
St. John, xxi. 16.

And other sheep I have, that are not of this fold; them also I must bring, and they shall hear my voice, and there shall be one fold and one shepherd.
St. John, x. 10.

VOL. I.

NO. 12.

SHEPHERD OF THE VALLEY.

...UIS, MISSOURI.

("ONE LORD, ONE FAITH, ONE BAPTISM.")

SEPTEMB...

SHEPHERD OF THE VALLEY,
PUBLISHED WEEKLY BY
FRANCIS H. TAYLOR.

...2 dollars per annum in advance.

...ns must be post paid, and addressed to the Editor.

...3rd, Street, Old Hospital building.

...monstrated by its continued succession. ...s, that the church now in communion with the ...is the only true church of God: which we

The Argument.

That is the only true church of God which ...tinued succession from Christ and his Apos... ...ne.

But the church now in communion with the ...and no other, has had a continued succession ...nd his Apostles to this time.

...ion. Therefore the church now in commun... ...ce of Rome, and no other, is the true church ...of first proposition is ...

ples, which neither our forefathers, nor we have been a- ble to bear? Acts 15. 7, 8. 9, 10.

S. James, who was bishop of the place, seconding by his sentence what Peter had decreed. All the multitude, saith S. Hierome, held their peace, and into his (Peter's) sentence, James the Apostle, and all the Priests did pass together, Epist. 89. to August. c. 2. Peter, saith he in the same place, was Prince and Author of the Decree. That S. Peter translated his Chair from Antioch to Rome, is proved. First, because he remained not always at An- tioch, as all that church acknowledgeth, nor did it ever challenge the first Chair in any General Council, as ap- pears in the Councils. Secondly, by the decrees of coun- cils, other Fathers, giving the primacy to the Roman Church.

The Council of Sardis, An. Dom. 400. Western Fa- thers 300. Eastern 76, decreed, that in cases of Bishops, for the honor of S. Peter's memory, it should be lawful to appeal from whatsoever other bishop to the bishop of Rome, Can. 3.

The council of Calcedon, Ann. Dom. 451. Fathers 600. We truly consider that all primacy and chief honour, ac- cording to the Canon, is to be kept for the arch-bishop of Old Rome. Section 16. And in the relation of the said council to Pope Leo, we have confirmed, say they, the rule ...

many Drunkards, Liars, Sorcerers, Sabbath-b... Characters of the basest sort in her union?

[It is ten thousand pities, but it will app... strange if we consider that Protestant Englan... tains more drunkards, thieves and robbers, th... lic countries put together!]

What a visible, grand, contradistinguishin... be found between her and the Apostolic churc... the Scriptures, and let your own conscienc... you in this matter.

[Poh! She is herself the Apostolic church ...visible grand contradiction you are getting ... your ignorance of this fact.]

Again you ask why not exercise those prer... which the Redeemer endowed you. These ... I suppose to be what holy Mother holds hers... dowed with; such as the power of establish... tions, to try Heretics, to punish, torture, an... who will not submit to her *absurd doctrines.* ...who came into this world, not to destroy men... save them, give you that minority, or sup... your fellow mortals? Is this the fruit wh... the long suffering Jesus produced? Is this ...

15. Masthead of an 1832 edition of the *Shepherd of the Valley,* Catholic news- paper published in St. Louis.

16. The Massachusetts "Nunnery Committee" was lampooned by a contemporary cartoonist.

17. Roger Brooke Taney, first Catholic in a presidential cabinet and as Chief Justice of the United States Supreme Court.

18. Catholic Bible Burning: falsehoods like this were used against John Hughes when the New York prelate protested forcing Catholic school children to read a Protestant Bible.

19. Archbishop John Hughes of New York (1797-1864).

20. Archbishop Gaetano Bedini, though beset by anti-Catholic mobs throughout his United States visit, returned to Rome to help found the North American College.

21. The Washington Monument was intended to include a stone from Pope Pius IX, but this gift was thrown in the Potomac River by an anti-Catholic mob.

22. Monument in the National Capital to "Nuns of the Battlefield," in recognition of their services during the War between the States.

A BOTTLE

AN ADOPTED CITIZEN

COMBINATION

Life, 1884

In the best of times, more or less unflattering stereotypes colored American attitudes toward immigrant minorities. The Irishman and the Jew stood out most sharply during the post-Civil War decades. The former invariably displayed a pug nose, an underslung jaw, and an air of tattered truculence, usually augmented by whiskey. The Jew was a symbol of mercenary cunning or vulgar social-climbing. Here "Mr. Moses Lichtenstein" is aping the "Four Hundred."

Life, 1889

23. Irishman, pugnacious under the stimulus of whiskey, was a popular caricature which reflected odium on the Church because of the renowned faith of the Sons of Erin.

24. Chaplain Patrick J. Ryan in this picture had become Archbishop of Philadelphia.

25. Pierre-Jean DeSmet, S.J., most famous of all missionaries to the American Indians.

ROMISH POLITICS—ANY THING TO BEAT GRANT.

26. Romish Politics: an example of Thomas Nast's anti-Catholic cartoons, depicting a wolfish Irishman with a priest lurking in the background.

27. General Charles Ewing, first Catholic Commissioner for Indian Missions.

28. Orestes A. Brownson, lecturer and author, who has been termed the most important American convert to the Church in the 19th century.

29. Archbishop John Ireland of St. Paul. This Irish-born prelate was distinguished for his Americanism from his consecration in 1875 until his death in 1918.

Courtesy New York Public Library

29. "'THE PROMISED LAND' AS SEEN FROM THE DOME
OF SAINT PETER'S, ROME"

31. "The Promised Land": perennial favorite in anti-Catholic propaganda are the alleged papal designs on the United States.

PUBLIC SCHOOLS MUST AND ALL BE PRESERVED. "FORT SUMTER." THE MAN THAT HAULS DOWN OUR PUBLIC SCHOOLS SHOOT HIM ON THE SPOT.

30. "Fort Sumter": anti-Catholic societies struck at the parochial school system by pretending the Church opposed the public schools.

32. Henry F. Bowers, founder and first supreme president of the American Protective Association.

THE HOME OF THE MENACE, AURORA, Mo. *Neg. No. 1.* ©1913 by R.E Hinchey, Aurora, Mo.

THE MENACE

THE MENACE

Home of The Menace, Aurora, Mo., U. S. A. ©1915 By R.E.Hinch

33. These 1913 and 1915 photographs of the plant of *The Menace* show growth
in 2 years. The original building had been enlarged and another one added.

34. James Cardinal Gibbons, Archbishop of Baltimore, 1877-1921.

35. This representation of Smith as the servant of the Catholic hierarchy appeared in *The Fellowship Forum,* November 3, 1928. It is typical of the extreme anti-Catholic Klan propaganda.

36. "Fiery Cross" of the Ku Klux Klan in the hands of a Cyclops (head of a local "den").

37. Dr. Hiram Wesley Evans, Imperial Wizard of the Knights of the Ku Klux Klan.

38. One of the Klan cartoons of 1928.

39. This much-used cartoon piles up many objections to Smith's candidacy, among which the symbol of his religion is the only one left unlabeled.

40. Alfred E. Smith. The Catholic Governor of New York was the Democratic presidential candidate in 1928.

41. Konrad Adenauer, Catholic Chancellor of West Germany's Federal Republic.

42. Myron C. Taylor, Personal Representative of the President at the Vatican, 1940-1950.

Picture Source Credits

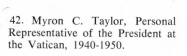

St. Louis Public Library Art Dept., 1, 4, 5, 6, 9, 17, 29. Michael Williams, *The Shadow of the Pope,* Whittlesey House, 2, 3, 14, 38. New York Historical Society, 8. N.C.W.C. Photo, 10, 11, 12, 22, 28, 34, 41, 42. St. Louis *Review,* 7, 15, 35. Reuben Maury, *The Wars of the Godly,* Robert M. McBride & Co., 13, 19, 32, 37, 40. Ray Allen Billington, *The Protestant Crusade,* Rinehart & Co., Inc., 16, 18. Robert F. McNamara, *The American College in Rome,* The Christopher Press, 20. Abbie Rowe photo—courtesy National Park Service, 21. John Higham, *Strangers in the Land,* Rutgers University Press, 23, 36. John Rothensteiner, *History of the Archdiocese of St. Louis,* Blackwell-Wielandy Co., 24, 25. New York Public Library, 26, 30, 31. Charles Ewing, 27. R. E. Hinchey, 33. New York State Library, 39.

Copyright, 1961, Franciscan Herald Press, 1434 West 51st Street, Chicago 9, Illinois putable . . . the ultimate consequence of this principle fully carried out is anarchy." Unfortunately Philadelphia had not seen the end of the total acceptance of the teaching of Jean Jacques Rousseau.

Two months later the noise of the Independence Day celebrations in this "Cradle of Liberty" resembled more the silence of the tomb when compared with the days immediately following. The evening of July 5 a crowd of nativists converged on the Church of St. Philip Neri in Southwark, a Philadelphia suburb like Kensington. Deterred by the arrival of the military from taking any action, the crowd congregated again the following day. But the knowledge that the militia had orders to fire were an assault made prevented anything more than sullen threats.

One disturber was arrested and imprisoned in the church by the military. The next day was Sunday and it need not be said that Mass was not offered in St. Philip Neri. By this time the mob had ripped two cannons from ships at the docks. These were dragged to the church doors and the fuses lit, but wet powder foiled the engines of destruction. Sunday afternoon more militia were called because of the increasing ugliness and size of the crowd. Finally actual warfare broke out, with the cannons being fired at the soldiers and the military replying with their muskets. By the lowest estimate 13 people were killed and more than 50 wounded. Thousands of Catholic families fled Philadelphia, and martial law was in force for weeks in the city.

"A SECOND MOSCOW"

Public indignation and horror was widespread at the anarchy of the nativist riots in Philadelphia. But a similar revulsion had taken place after the burning of the Charlestown convent, and yet the mob spirit had not been quenched. Actually bloody barbarities had increased; why were they to end at Philadelphia? It was Bishop John Hughes of New York who shored up a solid foundation upon which reasoned public opinion could stand unshaken.

When reports of the first riot in Philadelphia's suburb of Kensington reached New York, nativists there lit the fires for similar action. A huge mass meeting was called for Central Park. Bishop Hughes was not intimidated. When Napoleon in 1812 reached Moscow the retreating Russians burned the city as they left. Referring to this method of defense, Hughes publicly declared: "If a single Catholic church were burned in New York, the city would become a second Moscow." His quick investigation revealed that New York state law provided no compensation for churches burned by rioters. The bishop then warned the mayor that Catholic property would be protected.

Bishop Hughes did not leave actual self-preservation to impromptu action, but quickly stationed up to 2,000 armed men around each church. Realizing that such measures were dangerous in themselves, the bishop utilized the *Freeman's Journal and Catholic Register* to rush instructions that no Catholic was to strike the first blow. If attack came, however, they were to take as many lives as necessary before giving up their own for the cause of liberty. How tremendous was the influence of Bishop Hughes! Not a single defender, however impetuous, moved against the nativists. On the other hand, the sight of the determined sentinels quelled all plans the agitators may have devised. No incident of any kind took place in New York during May, 1844, nor again after the second bloody outbreak in Philadelphia during the following July.

This rocklike determination of John Hughes was not a sudden impulse. Born in Ireland of good family, he had not permitted a financial disaster to thwart his ambition to become a priest. On coming to America he had taken any kind of job to earn his tuition in the seminary. After he was ordained for the Diocese of Philadelphia, he led in adopting various methods to quiet the storm of anti-Catholicism. Reminiscent of the path followed by John Henry

Newman from the Episcopal ministry to the Catholic Church, he had founded a Catholic Tract Society in 1827 to publish booklets explaining the Faith.

In these years debates became more popular than pamphlets. In 1832 Hughes accepted the challenge of the Reverend John Breckinridge, a Philadelphia Presbyterian pastor. It was agreed that each contestant would publish articles alternately in *The Presbyterian* and in a Catholic paper. There being no Catholic publication at all in the Pennsylvania city, Father Hughes raised the money himself and commenced the *Catholic Herald* in January of 1833. Opinions of commentators on the outcome of the debate varied much according to their prior inclinations, but undoubtedly the energy and ability demonstrated by Hughes contributed to his selection as bishop in New York.

ANTI-CATHOLIC TEXTBOOKS

Particularly in New York City the new bishop found that the King James version of the Bible was being read to public-school pupils, usually followed by a commentary abusive of the Catholic Church. Moreover, the textbooks used not only were highly sympathetic to Protestantism but blatantly ridiculed Catholicism. Hughes reasoned that children from even solidly Catholic homes would be shaken in their faith from constantly hearing repeated such a phrase as "deceitful Catholics," to quote one of the least offensive terms.

Though he was promptly labeled as an enemy of the Bible, the bishop sought allocation of the school funds for construction of separate Catholic institutions. If that would not be granted, he asked that Catholic pupils study the Douay version (a Catholic translation) of Holy Scripture. Hughes was excoriated so soundly that neither political party would promise relief of any kind. The bishop then took the bold step of entering a Catholic ticket in a school election and its vote was sufficient to cause the Democrats to lose. Neither the city nor the state legislature ever accepted the proposals Hughes had made. Nevertheless, victory in part came when the reading of the Protestant Bible was dropped in many municipal schools.

During the summer of 1960 a popular national magazine compared John Hughes unfavorably with other Catholic prelates who later attained national distinction similar to his. That this Bishop (later Archbishop) of New York was a vigorous and forthright individual is absolutely true. But suavity and unction would have made no impress on either the leaders or the mobs who in his days were violently anti-Catholic. A time comes when force must be met with force and John Hughes had the courage and simplicity to use it. Their appetites whetted by the blood spilled in Philadelphia, the agitators who rushed to New York in 1844 would never have listened to words, however persuasive. But the armed resistance of the church guardians whom Bishop Hughes had marshalled slowed their malevolent rush to a sedate walk. This smoke-blackened decade for American Catholics had commenced with the destruction of the Charlestown convent. It ended abruptly with the burning of the churches in Philadelphia. It ceased so quickly because John Hughes from his cup of American citizenship had drunk deeply the invigorating red wine of American courage.

Chapter XII

THE RISE AND DECLINE OF KNOW-NOTHINGISM

PUBLIC REVULSION TO NATIVIST ATTACKS AND THE STURDY DE-
fense against them, particularly by New York Catholics, brought
comparative peace to the Church in the United States during the
late 1840's. Why was the tranquil sea of American life disturbed by
a squall more tempestuous than most of the previous storms? It
was probably due to a combination of the many causes cited
rather than to any certain one.

A few months after he became archbishop, John Hughes proclaimed in St. Patrick's Cathedral: "There is no secret about this.
The object we hope to accomplish in time, is to convert all pagan
nations and all Protestant nations. . . ." As late as 1960 in a popular magazine the archbishop was called arrogant for his statement.
Yet in itself it was hardly sufficient to have aroused sustained attack. The eminent position of the Archbishop of New York must
have been generally recognized, for President Polk had asked him
to be our nation's envoy to Mexico four years previously.

Nativist agitation was inflamed by any increase in immigration. Famine in Ireland and a suppressed revolution in Prussia had
filled incoming ships with newcomers to America. Animate beings,
however, were not required to infuriate some. For the Washington

101

monument then under construction, Pope Pius IX sent a block of African marble. To the anti-Catholic faction the advent of one of the ten plagues would have been more welcome. Diatribes from press and platform culminated in a mob seizing the stone and hurling it into the Potomac River. Hatred of the Church and not the injection of sectarianism must have been the motive. Otherwise, in climbing to the top of the monument, this writer's eyes would not have encountered at virtually every step a stone inscribed from some chapter of the Masonic Order or other organizations not noted for friendship to Catholics.

If the avowed enemies of the Church were incensed at the Pope's gift to all Americans, their rage approached the rabid in March of 1853. The newly elected Franklin Pierce named James Campbell, a Pennsylvania Catholic, to be United States Postmaster-General. The President was reviled, his nominee abused, and the country untruthfully warned that the Jesuits would have access to every letter in the mails. As Andrew Jackson had stood firm when an anti-Catholic outburst greeted his appointment of Catholic Roger B. Taney to the Supreme Court, Pierce was as unshakeable as the granite of his native New Hampshire. Campbell retained his post throughout the administration. Americans of a century ago were grateful to him for introducing perforated borders to stamps, so that no longer was a knife or scissors necessary to separate them.

The bedlam aroused by this Cabinet appointment had scarcely subsided when a fresh outburst commenced. Our country then had formal diplomatic relations with the Holy See, and when the Papal Nuncio to Brazil, Archbishop Gaetano Bedini, visited the United States he paid a courtesy call to President Pierce. Then commenced a tour of a country entirely new to him. Agitators preceded him from city to city and dogged his footsteps whenever he stopped. Riots became commonplace to him. The worst of the outbreaks disgraced Christmas night in Cincinnati. A mob of 600 stormed the residence of Archbishop John Baptist Purcell, where the Italian prelate was a guest. A newspaper account stated there were "some with torches to set fire to the cathedral and some with ropes with which to hang the Nuncio." One was killed and more than 50 injured before the police courageously quelled the onslaught.

ENEMIES ORGANIZE

When Archbishop Bedini returned to New York another mob was being collected to harass — at the very least — his departure. Had the doughty Archbishop John Hughes not been away for his health, that intrepid prelate probably would have stared down any potential rioters. In his absence the metropolitan clergy thought discretion the better course. Instead of from a tumultuous dock, Archbishop Bedini boarded his outgoing liner from a steam tug as the vessel passed through the Staten Island Narrows. Notwithstanding all this, this Italian Archbishop was so instrumental in erecting the North American College in Rome for the education of American ecclesiastics that he is considered a founder of the institution.

All these outbursts were not impulsive. By no means! By the time Archbishop Bedini left in 1854 anti-Catholicism in the United States was more fully organized than ever before. The cancer of exaggerated nationalism and hatred of fellow citizens because of their religion had for a time been recessive. The inflammation was ready to erupt and splotch the book of history with its corruption.

Had the outburst been spontaneous, it could have been presumed that the fault lay much with individual Catholics in various parts of the country. The few outrages just related of the many which took place were of an entirely different sort. They represented the planned maneuvers of a new organization which had evolved during the years of comparative calm. Anti-Catholicism had abandoned armed forays after public distaste had been so manifest following the Philadelphia riots of 1844. The Native American Party had collapsed but the seeds were ready again to bring forth weeds whenever the climate was agreeable.

SHROUDED IN SECRECY

Order of the Star Spangled Banner is a name which would imply profession of the virtues of patriotism and justice. Still it was from this nativist organization that a powerful political assault against Catholicism was made. At first the new political party bore no name, had no visible organization, and its emblem was not entered on any ballot. Secrecy enshrouded it further with the use of passwords, special grips for handshakes, mysterious signs of recognition between members, and esoteric signals of distress. Years later in his *Memoirs* former President Grant revealed that he had become a member solely to learn the inner secrets.

What was the name? The response of the members in the early 1850's was "I know nothing about it." From this standard reply evolved the popular designation: "Know-Nothings." And Know-Nothings they remained while the membership grew from an insignificant nativist group to a multitude which threatened to gain control of the national as well as state governments.

Operating through the American Party, the Know-Nothings in 1854 elected nine Governors, eight U.S. Senators and almost half of the membership of the national House of Representatives. Massachusetts is an example of the Know-Nothing domination of a commonwealth. The Governor, every member of the Senate, all of the state executives were Know-Nothings; and the state Assembly contained one Whig, one Free-Soiler, and 376 Know-Nothings.

The Know-Nothings were highly successful in using street preachers to liven the glowing embers of anti-Catholicism. In

Providence, Brooklyn, and on into the Midwest the technique proved effective. Though Archbishop Peter Richard Kenrick willingly allowed a church and St. Louis University to be searched for alleged arms and ammunition, the falsity of the charge did not quiet the mob. The St. Louis *Evening News* of August 9, 1854, reported in part: "For 48 hours the city has been the scene of one of the most appalling riots that has ever taken place in the country. Men have been butchered like cattle, property destroyed, and anarchy reigns supreme." A scene in Louisville the following year is typical.

"BLOODY MONDAY"

In the Kentucky city George D. Prentice filled his Louisville *Journal* with violent editorials supporting the Know-Nothing Party in an election of August, 1855. By noon on election day cries of "Down with the Dutch and Irish!" had been supplanted by thugs roving the streets with clubs. Six years before the Civil War this border city appeared to be besieged, as flames shot skyward in districts inhabited by immigrants. A mother rushed forth from the flames that were consuming her husband—but her dash was in vain. A maniac murdered in her arms the child she was carrying to safety. At least 20 persons were killed before "Bloody Monday" ended in Louisville.

The Catholic newspaper of Boston, *The Pilot,* gloomily feared that a Know-Nothing would be elected President in 1856. The candidate finally chosen by the party was Millard Fillmore, who had previously occupied this supreme executive position after Zachary Taylor died in office. At the time of his selection Fillmore was in Rome seeking an audience with Pope Pius IX. Though he accepted the nomination, Fillmore did not personally participate in the invectives hurled against the Church during the campaign. Almost 25 per cent of the popular vote was garnered by this nativist party, but its electoral vote was limited to the eight of Maryland.

ATTENTION DIVERTED

The nation's attention was being diverted by increasing tension between North and South. Actually the very success of the Know-Nothing Party was already bringing about its downfall. In Massachusetts, where the entire state government was in its hands, the members of the legislature were so inept that they were unable to pass laws against the Church they were committed to exterminate. Requiring voters to pass a literacy test was the sole enactment. A "Nunnery Committee" was appointed and conducted an "inquisition" of a Catholic school in Roxbury. After the members had disrupted the school, frightened the children, and boorishly refused to remove their hats while inspecting the chapel, they were forced to report that nothing could be found deserving of criticism. To climax the day's entertainment for the committee, a riotous dinner was held at which copious quantities of champagne were consumed at public expense in a state in which sale of the beverage was illegal. These and other unreportable escapades of the group were so notorious that its chairman was expelled from the Massachusetts Assembly.

Meanwhile secrecy, once a lure to the adventurous, became odious as the party sought power and responsibility. Thinking citizens could not long be credulous of ridiculous charges of a "Popish" plot to invade the United States. Once members had glorified in the name "Know-Nothing." They shamefully withdrew as pseudo-organizations espoused the titles of "Owe-Nothing," and "Do-Nothing."

Four years later in the 1860 election the Know-Nothings were absorbed in the Constitutional Union Party, which ran last in the divided contest of that momentous year. An abortive attempt to revive the so-called American Party in 1880 was ineffectual. In the entire country its total vote numbered 707! Once again both the United States and the Catholic Church had survived a test. A political party founded on hatred of fellow Americans had been rejected and exterminated.

Chapter XIII

CATHOLIC PATRIOTISM WON FRIENDS DURING THE CIVIL WAR

INCREASED ATTENTION HAS BEEN GIVEN RECENTLY TO ALEXIS de Tocqueville. After his visit to the United States in the 1830's this Frenchman wrote so penetratingly of democracy in America that even the exaggerated adulation of Henry Adams could not tarnish the worth of his writings. Within a couple of years after the death of this scholarly statesman further demonstration had come of his declaration: "The Catholics of the United States are at the same time the most faithful believers in God and the most zealous citizens of the Republic."

The first opportunity for Catholics to establish their loyalty to America had come during the Revolution from England; already we have seen how splendidly that test was met. The passage of almost "fourscore and seven years" had dimmed for some the remembrance of the glorious record of Catholics during the American Revolution. Nativists had come not only to question their loyalty but their very eligibility to become true citizens. Not by words but by deeds—this time "in a great Civil War"—Catholics vindicated De Tocqueville's judgment of their being the best of citizens.

108

SIXTY-NINTH REGIMENT

Three days after the first shot was fired at Fort Sumter President Lincoln called for 75,000 volunteers. New York's Sixty-Ninth Regiment was the first to respond. Within 48 hours these soldiers, mostly young Irish Catholic men, were on their way to the front.

Five years of potato famine in Ireland and heartless eviction by English landlords had brought thousands of impoverished Irish immigrants to the United States in the decade preceding the Civil War. Due to the difference in the size of the cities the influx of the sons of Erin had been ever more noticeable in Boston than in New York. Often landing absolutely destitute, Irish boys and even girls had eagerly accepted any sort of work. The 50,000 and more in the Hub City had crowded into the North End and Fort Hill. Soon it became almost a proverb to say that a good workman did as much as an Irishman. Notwithstanding, the Puritan social and financial aristocracy despised these newcomers. Unable to understand their deep loyalty to Catholicism, an eminent historian has criticized the Boston Irish for refusing to take jobs distant from "the ministrations of their priests." Oppressed for their religion in Erin, the spiritual sons of St. Patrick encountered similar opposition when searching for work in Boston by signs which read: "No Irish Need Apply."

These placards were hurriedly removed because of the unflinching loyalty of the Irish Catholics to their newly adopted country. General Burnside erred grievously in attacking Lee's impregnable position at Fredericksburg. But for the Gaelic members of the Irish Brigade, "their's not to reason why, their's but to do and die." A correspondent for the London *Times* marveled at the "undaunted courage displayed by the Sons of Erin" as they made seven successive stormings of the invincible position from

which the Confederates poured forth shot and shell. Two-thirds
of General Thomas Meagher's Brigade never again answered roll
call. They had not died in vain. No nativist back in Boston dared
question the love of the Irish Catholics for their new-found homeland.

Highly important to the Union was preventing European nations from allying with the South or recognizing the Confederacy
as independent. In October, 1861, Archbishop John Hughes of
New York was invited to Washington. There President Lincoln
commissioned him to present the position of the Union to the
Catholic Emperor of France, Napoleon III. After he had disem-
barked at Liverpool the Archbishop stated his intention in a letter
to a Cardinal in Rome:

> I made known to the President that if I should come to
> Europe, it would not be as a partisan of the North more
> than of the South; that I should represent the interests of
> the South as well as the North—in short, the interests of
> all the United States, just the same as if they had never
> been distracted by the presence of a war.

On Christmas Eve at the Tuileries Hughes had a long conversation
with Napoleon and the Empress Eugenie. As a consequence
France neither intervened in the struggle nor accorded official
recognition to the Confederacy.

PACIFIES RIOTERS

In his numerous letters to Secretary of State William Seward,
Archbishop Hughes mentioned visiting European spas in the hope
that the baths might revive his health. On his return to America it
was evident that not many days were left to him. Notwithstanding,
he made one more effort to aid his adopted country. Volunteers

having become insufficient, Congress enacted the country's first draft law in 1863. When the initial names were being drawn in New York, the city was immobilized by a riot which lasted four days. The poor had revolted against enforcement because the regulations permitted an exemption to be purchased for $300.00 and because foreign labor was being imported to keep wages from rising.

At the height of the melee the governor appealed to Hughes to pacify the insurrectionists. Physically incapable of even standing, the Archbishop had notices posted inviting the rioters to come to his residence. Seated in a chair on a balcony, the Archbishop pleaded with his listeners to cease the commotion. Having given his blessing, Archbishop Hughes retired from what was his last public appearance. Three days after the New Year began this valiant Irish-American churchman and patriot breathed his last.

During the War with Mexico President Polk had provided for a few Catholic chaplains. After the War between the States commenced Lincoln wrote Archbishop Hughes. The President stated he could find no law governing hospital chaplains, but "I will thank you to give me the name or names of one or more suitable persons of the Catholic Church" who would be appointed for that purpose. Among the priests who served in the Union forces several became distinguished prelates, such as Archbishop John Ireland of St. Paul and Bishop Lawrence McMahon of Hartford. Patrick J. Ryan, later Coadjutor Bishop of St. Louis and Archbishop of Philadelphia, resigned his chaplaincy because he felt he could do better work in the hospital among Southern prisoners of war as a volunteer priest. Many others proffered their services as the need arose. When there was no priest at all in Fredericksburg, though "the city is literally a hospital," Bernard McQuaid went there from Newark, N. J., to attend the dying. The future first Bishop of Rochester, N. Y. remained until another priest was assigned.

In the South the clergy were not at first exempt from conscription. Bishop Patrick N. Walsh of Charleston having protested, priests were then assigned as chaplains for the Confederate forces. Among them was Francis Xavier Leray, later Archbishop of New Orleans. Abram Ryan, poet-priest of the South, was a volunteer chaplain amid the fighting in the West. In a gallant attempt to obtain foreign assistance Bishop Walsh evaded the northern naval blockade and crossed the Atlantic. His perilous voyage was in vain, for by then Europe recognized that the cause of the valiant men in gray was lost.

Probably the Church derived most benefit from the services of the members of the various Sisterhoods. Early in 1862 the Union Government requested that Sisters be assigned as nurses. To many Americans women in religious orders or congregations were something entirely unknown. Those who saw them on duty, and especially all who benefited from their tender care, never again would listen to any calumny directed against these dedicated women.

MONUMENT TO SISTERS

Especially at Gettysburg did Sisters win the title, "Angels of the Battlefield." From nearby Emmitsburg Sisters of Charity were taken in wagons over muddy roads to care for the fifty thousand killed and wounded on both sides. One unforgettable scene was sister Petronilla Breen sitting on a shattered tree stump making compresses from strips of material she had torn from garments of her own which she had brought.

William Tecumseh Sherman was not beloved in the South after his march through Georgia. But Sisters at Charleston found him both gracious and understanding when they sought to take their orphan charges from that besieged city. No doubt remembering his own Catholic wife, Sherman appointed a military escort for the Sisters and the little children in this evacuation effort. Later the Union General visited the religious and their pupils.

In 1914 the Ladies Auxiliary of the Ancient Order of Hibernians petitioned for a monument in the national capital to the Sisters who served during the Civil War. Ten years were spent in gathering authentic data. The official records revealed that more than 600 Sisters had been enrolled in service, plus many unrecorded volunteers. The monument to the "Nuns of the Battlefield" was unveiled in Washington on September 20, 1924. It stands today opposite the entrance to St. Matthew's Cathedral as the nation's tribute to these devoted women.

Drear days would come again for the Church in America, but there would be no basis for criticism of Catholic loyalty. The patriotism of the faithful had met the supreme test in battle and proved true and unyielding. Again the God of peace had drawn good out of war.

Chapter **XIV**

BIGOTRY IN HIGH PLACES DURING THE RECONSTRUCTION PERIOD

NO PUBLIC ACCLAMATION OF THE VALOROUS PARTICIPATION OF Catholics was uttered by the Federal Government after General Lee's surrender at Appomattox; the voice of the prostrate South was throbbing too low to be heard on any subject. Catholics had prized the public commendation of President Washington on their courageous contribution to the success of the American Revolution. Perhaps it was a mark of the progress of the Church that after the Civil War her members were not singled out for praise. By 1865 most Americans recognized that their Catholic fellow citizens would do their part for God and country.

THE CHURCH AND THE INDIANS

If anti-Catholicism was dormant during the Reconstruction Era among the general run of people, by no means had it disappeared entirely. There was no recurrence of the Know-Nothing period when mobs were aroused to an unreasoning fury against the Church by harangues on street corners. The bigotry was in high places. In a sense the opposition was directed against the Church fulfilling the final commission received from our divine Lord while He was on this earth: "Go, therefore, and make dis-

114

ciples of all nations" (Matt. 28:19).

Unacquainted with the true God, the American Indian was a perfect subject for the fulfillment of Jesus' command. Restricting our attention to the English colonies, settlement and conversion were twin objectives in the Catholic colony of Maryland. Before a landing was made the consent of the Piscataway tribe was obtained; soon almost all of these redmen were converted to Catholicity. The civilizing influence of Christianity was early recognized by the Federal Government. During Washington's administration $200 was allotted annually to two Catholic Indian missionaries. An agreement with the War Department to conduct a school for Indian boys brought the Jesuits to Missouri in 1823. Among the group was Pierre-Jean DeSmet, who became the most famous of all apostles to the redmen. Years later came dramatic proof that the redskins recognized him as the ambassador of the Prince of Peace. After Sitting Bull had sworn to kill the first white man he saw, Father DeSmet visited him alone and obtained a peace treaty.

But the Indian was bound to be disturbed as settlers continued to push into lands which had been promised to him "as long as grass grows and water flows." In his message to Congress on December 5, 1870, President Ulysses S. Grant offered a new approach. The President's own words: "I determined to give all the agencies to such religious denominations as had hitherto established missionaries among the Indians . . . ." Already some reservations had been entrusted to the care of the Society of Friends. With that assignment there scarcely could have been any quarrel, for the Quakers had followed the Catholics of Maryland in treating the Indians fairly.

INDIAN BUREAU HOSTILE

When the plan—soon known as Grant's Peace Policy—was announced, Catholics hailed it with enthusiasm. With a record of continuous care of the aborigines since 1634, it appeared that the problem of the Church would be staffing all the reservations which would be allotted. No such difficulty arose. Out of approximately 80 agencies only seven were assigned to the Church. The Indians living on these particular reservations numbered about 17,000. In contrast, such latecomers in the evangelization of the Indians as the Methodists were entrusted with 54,000 tribesmen.

One by one western bishops made trips to Washington they could ill afford. Vague and indefinite promises were the most any prelate obtained, and none of these were fulfilled. As months added into years the hostility to the Church of executives of the Indian Bureau became more evident. A Paulist priest's intercession offered a happy method of circumventing them. Before his own conversion to Catholicism and study for the priesthood this George Deshon had been both classmate and roommate of Ulysses Grant at West Point. The chief executive received him in the national capital and at his summer home in Long Branch, New Jersey. His reception was so cordial that Deshon reported with enthusiasm: "We will have all the agencies in which the Indians are Catholic." The Paulist was to return to his previous assignment considerably chastened in spirit. Not a single one of Grant's pledges was executed!

Perhaps improvement could be effected through permanent representation in the national capital? That proposal seemed unobtainable because of lack of money to finance it. In 1873 Charles Ewing volunteered to be a lay apostle. The non-Catholic father of this Ohioan had been in two presidential cabinets, and during the Civil War Ewing had risen to the rank of General. As a successful Washington attorney he accepted the position of Catholic Indian Commissioner, continuing in the office without a single cent of compensation until his death in 1883.

Aided by a veteran Indian missionary named Father Jean-Baptiste Abraham Brouillet, Ewing promoted the education of

Indian children. Here Catholic teachers excelled where those of Protestant denominations failed abjectly. Yet no other reservations were assigned to Catholics. In fact, priests were rigorously excluded from all agencies assigned to Protestants. To a Catholic Indian who asked for a "black robe" the agent on one reservation replied: "Washington has decided that you must get to heaven by the Episcopalian route."

STRIKE AT CATHOLIC SCHOOLS

Antagonism to the Church by the Indian Bureau may have been pronounced, but it was no isolated phenomenon. The "bloody shirt" the Republican Party had been waving since the Civil War became a bit ragged. In its stead some G.O.P. candidates substituted the Pope, a traditional punching bag for anti-Catholic pugilists. Rutherford B. Hayes won the Ohio governorship in 1875 by charging the Democrats with being the "Romanist" party. Haunted by his own words, Hayes, instead of repenting, resolved to smear the opposition with the same tar. As the presidential candidate the following year Hayes suggested to his advisor Carl Schurz that New York's withdrawal of accreditation from a school of the Grey Nuns be sounded against Governor Samuel J. Tilden, his Democratic opponent.

Hayes' tactics in Ohio in 1875 may have influenced Grant, who was receptive to a third-term offer. Addressing a veterans' convention in Des Moines that fall, the President scored private schools. His speech was interpreted as aimed at Catholic institutions. When Congress convened in December the first bill introduced in the House was a constitutional amendment striking at denominational schools. The Speaker, "silver-tongued" James G. Blaine, sponsored the measure and piloted it through the House of Representatives, but it failed to win approval of two-thirds of the Senators.

Meanwhile Chief Red Cloud of the Sioux had repeatedly begged for Catholic teachers and schools. As early as 1875 the Chicago *Times* had queried: "If the Indian asks for this kind of spiritual meat, why give him a stone?" In 1880 Bishop James O'Connor, Vicar Apostolic of Nebraska, determined on a test. A Benedictine priest named Meinrad McCarthy was sent to the reservation in Dakota Territory on which Red Cloud and his tribe were quartered. When the Indian Commissioner in Washington heard of his presence, he promptly telegraphed to expel him. Immediately Father McCarthy left to avoid a fine of $1,000.00 which neither he nor Bishop O'Connor could pay.

For six weeks the Benedictine camped on the prairie near the reservation. Meanwhile every brave and squaw on the reservation signed a petition to the President, begging that the priest be allowed to enter. Washington did not even deign to reply to the soul-stirring plea.

RELIGIOUS LIBERTY FOR INDIANS

After the expulsion of Father McCarthy from the Red Cloud Reserve representatives of the Protestant denominations participating in the Peace Policy were queried about admitting him. Every single one opposed granting to the Indian the freedom of conscience guaranteed by the Constitution. Late in 1880 an agent on a Catholic reservation carried out the directive of the Indian Bureau and expelled a Congregationalist minister. Now ten different Protestant denominations promptly protested. Early the following year the prohibition was rescinded. Catholics had won the fight for religious liberty for the Indian!

The Know-Nothings of the 1850's were the first major political party whose principal objective was fighting the Catholic church. Another anti-Catholic "first" was the attempted constitutional amendment of 1875 against Catholic schools. In the machinations of the Peace Policy came another unwelcome innovation in the open hostility of high government officials. Undismayed by prestige and power, Catholic leaders sought religious liberty for all Indians, as well as a rightful share of agency assignments. In the second respect failure was complete; years of striving brought not a single additional Indian reservation. Defeat it was, but however important it seemed at the time, today it must be admitted that no permanent harm was suffered. Religious liberty, on the contrary, is a fundamental right. Regaining freedom of conscience for the Indian was a tremendous achievement by the Church, and deserves to be numbered among the major glories of Catholics in America.

Chapter XV

CATHOLIC PRESTIGE RAISED BY WRITERS AND CHURCH COUNCILS

COLORADO BEING KNOWN AS THE "CENTENNIAL STATE" IS A CON-
stant reminder of the series of 100th anniversaries which the United
States commenced to celebrate in 1876. And it is not parenthetical
at all, but very pertinent, that this commonwealth resplendent in
natural wonders adopted for its motto "Nil Sine Numine" (Nothing Without God). Jubilees inevitably bring forth comparisons
of past with present, and with the nation the Catholic Church then
had multitudinous reasons for thanking God.

As the United States of 1876 was far more proud of that in-
definable Americanism than of multiplication of numbers and
expanse of boundaries, so the Church gloried in the intensity of
Catholicism more than growth and size. But if figures were to be
cited, those of the Church were even more impressive than the
totals for the nation of which she was a part.

SCHOLARLY CONVERTS

When Catholic Charles Carroll signed the Declaration of Independence only two buildings in the United States could actually
be called Catholic churches. Mass was offered in private homes for
fear of persecution. One hundred years later 5,000 Catholic

churches adorned the land. They were needed for the 6,000,000 faithful, a wondrous multiplication of the 15,000 valiant Catholics of the American Revolution. Then there had not been even a single parochial school; in the centennial year 63 colleges were happily combining secular and religious education.

One of the strongest voices for Catholic education in the 19th century came from a man who had never seen a Catholic school of any kind as a boy. But from childhood Orestes A. Brownson had sought to know the Almighty. Seeing soldiers drilling for the War of 1812 when he was about nine, on his return home he reported having heard two men talking about God. The discussion of eternity by two onlookers was more impressive to this child than soldiers resplendent in uniforms and muskets.

A satisfying knowledge of God did not come easily to the scintillating intellect of Brownson. First a Universalist minister, then a Unitarian preacher, he was hovering between atheism and agnosticism when he joined other New England intellectuals at Brook Farm. Long before the collapse of that experiment in communal life on a craggy Massachusetts hillside, Brownson had departed on his unceasing quest. The end of the long road was his instruction and baptism by the Coadjutor Bishop of Boston, John Bernard Fitzpatrick.

Shaking his pompadoured black hair from pulpit and platform, Brownson long since had established his reputation as a lecturer. But his powerful voice was not the equal of his more gifted pen. For years his *Quarterly Review* was eagerly awaited in Washington. He considered that part of his life terminated when he entered the Church. Bishop Fitzpatrick encouraged him to continue publication because of Catholicity's need of a bold champion. Later the *British Quarterly Review* admitted that "Brownson is the best of the Romish editors."

Many have hailed this broad-shouldered New Englander as

the most important convert of the last century. In 1865 Brownson discontinued his *Review* for a time to concentrate on his penetrating study, *The American Republic*. Fortunately that very year gave birth to another Catholic literary periodical whose merit also was recognized outside of the Church. There was a marked similarity to Brownson in its editor. Isaac Hecker likewise had been in the group at Brook Farm before his search ended in the Catholic Church. After he had been ordained a priest, he founded the Paulist Fathers to carry the Gospel to "other sheep not of this fold."

UNINTENDED COMPLIMENT

Recognizing that the printed page would reach some who would never hear the spoken word, Hecker began publication of the *Catholic World*. Though the circulation of this monthly publication was not large, its influence was so powerful that a new light dawned for the faithful. An unintended compliment was given in the founding of an organization called the American and Foreign Christian Union. Its declared purpose was to improve the literary output of Protestants in anti-Catholic publications. The title of its magazine, the *Christian World,* was too close for coincidence to Father Hecker's publication. Revenue for the first year was $138,-526.44. As was usual with publications founded on hatred, the gold mine petered out. By 1878 the annual income had dropped to one-thirteenth of the initial year.

Both in and outside the Church the educated felt the impact of the works of Brownson and Hecker. More Americans were aware that the Catholic hierarchy convened for the II Council of Baltimore in 1866. The rift between North and South had been paralleled by a like geographic split in most major Protestant denominations. The assembling of the prelates in Baltimore was an effective reminder that the Catholic Church had passed through the military and political separation entirely undivided in doctrine.

Moreover, spiritual allegiance to the Pope had not trammeled the patriotism of either northern or southern Catholics. The continued unity of the Church was a happy harbinger to the nation that the wounds of civil strife could be healed completely.

PERENNIAL "BEST SELLER"

An author's first book did as much for the Church as all other American publications of the 19th century combined. The keen bright eyes of James Gibbons were aided by the salutary assignments he had filled. As a young priest he had been a country pastor in Maryland. When Gibbons became the youngest bishop in the entire Catholic world in 1868 his charge was the State of North Carolina. At his episcopal consecration it had been called a "desert of Catholicity." But Gibbons loved and was loved by his people, and the same was true after his transfer to Virginia as Bishop of Richmond. The consequence of these years of thinking and preparation was the publication in the last days of the centennial year of *The Faith of Our Fathers.* Success was both astonishing and immediate! Within six months after publication the book already had sold through the fourth revised edition.

In the introduction the author had declared: "Should the perusal of this book bring one soul to the knowledge of the Church, my labor will be amply rewarded." Even more than in the number of copies was the work in this respect a "best seller." In receiving the Cardinal Gibbons Medal at the Catholic University of America, historian Carleton J. H. Hayes recalled that 50 years before he had been guided into the Church by *The Faith of Our Fathers.* An Irish well digger gave a copy to a woman for whom he was working, and she, too, joined the faithful. Ascribing his conversion to the same source, the former Protestant Episcopal Bishop of Delaware said: "I have come to see that the Roman Catholic Church is the best guarantee for preserving the Christian ideals of

American life." The appeal to people of such wide diversity of tastes and training is best accounted for by the compliment from a South Carolina pastor: "Everything in the book is as clear as a sunbeam." In all, more than 2,000,000 copies have been sold. Like Old Man River, *The Faith of Our Fathers* keeps rolling along nearly a hundred years after its initial release.

"RUM, ROMANISM AND REBELLION"

Less than a year after the publication of this book James Gibbons became Archbishop of the original see in this country, Baltimore. He left Protestant Virginia convinced, as he said, that the state was blessed with people who had "a broad religious toleration and a social fraternal spirit." Not many years after his elevation Archbishop Gibbons was appointed Apostolic Delegate for the III Plenary Council of Baltimore. It opened less than a week after Grover Cleveland was elected the first Democratic President since the outbreak of the Civil War. But a few days prior to the voting an incident had occurred which proved two things. First, the anti-Catholic spirit was not dead, despite Gibbons' pleasant experience in Virginia. Secondly, American Catholics had lost some of their submissiveness and when provoked were ready to assert themselves.

The occasion arose when a group of Republicans was presented to James G. Blaine, the confident G.O.P. candidate. Acting as spokesman, Presbyterian minister Samuel T. Burchard assured the nominee from Maine that we "don't propose to . . . identify ourselves with the party whose antecedents are rum, Romanism, and rebellion." Blaine did not repudiate the linking of Catholics with drunkards and revolutionaries, and Democrats immediately capitalized on the remark. A great-aunt of the writer related that handbill reminders were distributed outside St. Patrick's Cathedral in New York the following Sunday morning. With its important

Catholic population that state was carried by Cleveland by a little more than 1,000 votes, and thereby he became the national victor.

CATHOLIC SCHOOLS

The voice of the people having been heard, the 300 churchmen who convened in Baltimore the following Sunday ignored the incident completely. Among the 319 decrees of this Council, those on Catholic education showed the determination of the American hierarchy to expand and improve despite any opposition. In this year of 1884, some 500,000 children were attending parochial schools. This was the total Catholic population in the United States just 55 years earlier. The assembled bishops told the people that "no parish is complete until it has schools adequate to the needs of its children." They urged the faithful not to "relax their efforts till their schools be elevated to the highest educational excellence."

America had been honored in 1875 with the appointment of its first member in the College of Cardinals, Archbishop John McCloskey of New York. Too ill to attend the council in Baltimore, he died within the year. There could hardly have been a dissenting voice among the 9,000,000 Catholics then in the United States at the choice of his successor. The slight form of James Gibbons, a bit less than average in height, had grown in the mind's eye of the faithful to something akin to King St. Louis IX astride his charger. For 35 years His Eminence wore the red hat, gently but firmly guiding the Catholic Church in these United States.

Chapter XVI

VIOLENT OUTBREAKS CAUSED BY THE A.P.A.

WITH PERIODIC REGULARITY BUT WITH EVER-LESSENING VIRU-
lence, a flaming rash of anti-Catholicism has disfigured the usually
benign countenance of Uncle Sam. From the outbreak of the War
between the States his urbanity had been almost undisturbed. Then
in the 1890's a splotch became ever more livid until almost all of
his face was distorted. Why?

In the three-quarters of a century which has passed since that
canker receded from Uncle Sam's face, an answer to the question
has been sought. Catholic success with the Indians despite the
obstacles of Grant's Peace Policy, the III Plenary Council, and the
first Apostolic Delegate to the United States have been suggested
as irritants. More proximate to the outbreak of the sore was the
fourth centennial of the discovery of America by Columbus. To
those who had accepted the claim of a completely Protestant heritage without ever consulting history, that Columbus and his spon-
sor, Queen Isabella, were Catholics was a dismaying shock.

SEVEN FOUNDERS

For weal or woe organization is necessary. Unfortunately for
the Church a group was waiting in the wings of the American stage

for its cue. This newcomer, the American Protective Association, was spawned in 1887 at the railroad junction of Clinton, Iowa. With six others a 60-year-old lawyer named Henry T. Bowers fathered the A.P.A., as the organization was familiarly known throughout its life. Of the seven founders, two had no religion, while the other five were divided among as many different Protestant sects. An ardent Mason himself, Bowers drew heavily on that order for the regalia and initiation he devised for the A.P.A. Moreover, the Masons were a fertile source of new members or of allies.

After six years of slow growth under Bowers, the A.P.A. acquired a new president in William J. H. Traynor. A former saloonkeeper, Traynor was quickly tagged "Whiskey Bill," and it is true that he did inject new spirit in the organization. In Canada and later in Michigan Traynor had published anti-Catholic newspapers. Probably his experience had much to do with the increase in A.P.A. "scandal sheets," which by the following year numbered at least 70.

False charges against the Church and her members had been characteristic of every American anti-Catholic movement. The allegations oftentimes were ridiculous; still they seemingly originated from lack of knowledge rather than known lies. No such extenuation could be made of the literature of the 1890's. Two blatant forgeries were propagated on a national scale and for a time did great harm to the Church. The United States being plagued by the Panic of 1893, the A.P.A. published "Instructions to Catholics" supposedly signed by leading members of the hierarchy. This spurious document said that jobs were needed to support a mythical army, and "this will render it necessary to remove or crowd out the American heretics who are now employed." In the hard times this imposture callously increased the fears of those out of work or in danger of losing their jobs.

More outlandish—and more widely believed—was a bogus

encyclical letter of Pope Leo XIII, supposedly dated Christmas, 1891. First published by Traynor in his Detroit *Patriotic American,* this false papal letter absolved Catholics from any loyalty to the United States and instructed them "to exterminate all heretics" on September 5. Not only did every A.P.A. newspaper reprint the forgery, but it was broadcast even wider by handbills and leaflets. The mayor of Toledo bought a Winchester rifle to repel the invasion, but the panic was greatest among Midwestern farmers who had never known any of the faithful. When the date passed with no disturbance of any kind by Catholics, the A.P.A. press lied that it had been written by a Jesuit in order to discredit the A.P.A.

"A.P.A. BELT"

If all this was false, there was no question as to the increase in strength of the American Protective Association. Though large councils were in Boston and in San Francisco, the A.P.A. was strongest in the Midwest. In fact, newspapers of the time called the area from Ohio through Kansas and Nebraska "the A.P.A. Belt." In 1895 President Traynor boasted of 2,500,000 members. Most students of the movement believe his claim was highly exaggerated. But no final answer can be given, for secrecy was one of the inducements for many joining.

One of the frequent outbreaks brought on by lectures given by alleged ex-priests and nuns occurred in Kansas City, Missouri, in 1894. J. V. McNamara called himself "Bishop" and had a long record of involvement in riots as far east as New York. As his wife sold tickets for a Sunday night lecture a pistol was prominently displayed on the table beside her. When "Bishop" McNamara appeared on the platform he carried a revolver and a Winchester rifle. After two hours and more of abuse of the Church and local Catholics by McNamara, a stone landed on the stage. Later it was charged that a cohort of McNamara had dropped the rock in order to promote customers for a second lecture the following Tuesday.

Though the second performance was billed "For Men Only" all women who had the price of admission were allowed in the hall. McNamara launched an attack full of obscenity and filth on the venerable Bishop of Kansas City and two priests, one of whom succeeded as bishop some years later. The Kansas City *Star* acknowledged that McNamara's language could not be printed. For the riot which broke out the newspaper headline was, "He barely escaped alive." Though McNamara suffered little physical injury, he did not leave Kansas City unscathed. He was convicted of criminally libeling one of the priests, with the penalty a year in jail and a fine of $500. "The verdict was received with evidences of great dissatisfaction by the great crowd of members of the A.P.A.," reported the Kansas City *Star*. Notwithstanding, the "Bishop" and his supporters found that the freedom of speech guaranteed in the United States did not include license to slander.

MEMBERS REVEALED

Many inducted into the A.P.A. relied upon the clandestineness of membership to enable them to retain the business of Catholics. By striking this "heel of Achilles" two militant Catholic editors disrupted the organization in their territories. In the *Western Watchman* of St. Louis, Father David S. Phelan printed A.P.A. names for over three months in the fall of 1894. His scathing editorials continued until the once virulent yet virile body became a mute, riddled corpse.

Apparently the association had become even stronger in San Francisco when Father Peter C. Yorke was appointed editor of the *Monitor*. To obtain membership lists Father Yorke even engineered the admission of the *Monitor* reporters into the local lodges. Then names and addresses of members were emblazoned on the front page of his journal. Some who judiciously withdrew later subscribed to the *Monitor* to determine if business associates still belonged. Revealed adherence inflicted political leprosy, as successively local, area, and state candidates were defeated in California elections, after the *Monitor* disclosed their membership in the once-powerful A.P.A.

As much as anything else, the unwillingness of Americans long to stomach a diet of hatred brought the unlamented demise of the A.P.A. One effect lingered after its membership had dwindled to the vanishing point. In 1864 Congress had provided for a Hall of Statuary in the national capital, in which each state could place replicas of two distinguished sons. In 1673 the Jesuit Jacques Marquette had commenced and completed his journey of discovery down the Mississippi River in what is now the State of Wisconsin. More than 200 years later, in 1887, the state legislature voted to place Marquette's statue in Washington. When the sculptured figure was delivered in February, 1896, plans were ready for its official unveiling in March.

Special trains scheduled to leave Wisconsin for the ceremony never departed. William S. Linton of Michigan, known as the "A.P.A. spokesman in Congress," vituperated against acceptance of Marquette's statue. Though the House of Representatives was horrified at his language, no legislation was attempted because unanimous consent of Congress was required.

Through its journal, the *Wisconsin Patriot,* the A.P.A. then campaigned strenuously for the recall of the Jesuit explorer's likeness. Early in 1897 petitions pro and con descended on the state legislature like a winter snowstorm. But in the end a majority of the 423 petitions favored leaving Marquette's figure in Statuary Hall.

NEW ATTITUDE

Already the A.P.A. had begun to fade from the Wisconsin scene; in 1898 its newspaper expired. But politicians feared to arouse any latent strength, and no action was undertaken. The statue remained in Washington, still unauthorized but solidly present. Finally in 1904, 17 years after the original legislation, Congress accepted Marquette's statue for the Federal Government.

The A.P.A. aberration of the last decade followed the pattern of anti-Catholic outbreaks throughout the 19th century. If the assaults on the Rock of Peter were virtually identical, Catholic reaction of the 1890's was more militant, less submissive. Theodore Mommsen penned the dictum: "Walls and moats are of no avail, if a garrison will not fight." In addition, educated Americans who were not members of the Church were less prone to condone irresponsible attacks on her. Typical of the new attitude was Theodore Roosevelt, then New York City Police Commissioner. To his Catholic friends, the Bellamy Storers, he jocularly wrote: "As you know, I am a rather stiff-necked heretic . . ." but he assured them that if they felt any help was needed in Cincinnati "against the A.P.A., I will gladly come on." More than in the multiplication of numbers had the Catholics in America grown in public prestige during the 19th century.

Chapter XVII

CATHOLICS ARE SMEARED
BY "THE MENACE"

THE SPEEDY TRIUMPH OF THE UNITED STATES IN THE WAR WITH
Spain diverted attention from everything else. However, no dis-
traction was needed to insure the total collapse of the American
Protective Association. Bigotry and hatred of the Church had already palled the taste of almost all Americans. Once again in religion the United States was truly "the land of the free."

A distinct improvement in the position of the faithful was
apparent to the observant in 1898's brief conflict with a Catholic
nation. Historians generally attribute the resort to hostilities to the
insistent headlines of some segments of the press. Intent though
they were on building circulation, Hearst and Pulitzer newspapers
did not seek to arouse animosity toward the Spanish because they
were Catholics. Unlike in the War with Mexico fifty years before,
the churches of Cuba were not held forth as places to be pillaged
in the event of victory. Nor did Catholic soldiers have to listen to
preachings against the Church, as was true in 1846.

WIDE CIRCULATION

Some have contended that from the downfall of the A.P.A.
until after World War I the hydra of anti-Catholicism scarcely

132

took a deep breath in these United States. If the actual incidents were comparatively minor, their relation to postwar outbreaks should not be overlooked. The Kansas farmer who drills his wheat in the fall may use some of it for pasturage. The success of his crop, however, will not be determined by a particularly verdant stand before the snows come. The kernels in the heads waving in the golden fields late in June will give the answer. Our Lord spoke of bad fruit as well as good fruit, and an abundant harvest was to be gathered from the weeds which were sowed before and during World War I.

Envy is so dissatisfying a sin in that it benefits in no way. Yet the green-eyed monster had a ready champion in Thomas E. Watson of Georgia. His own emotionalism having made him successful as a trial lawyer, he became nationally known as a Populist in the 1890's. *Watson's Magazine* dwindled in circulation with the disintegration of this political party. His trumpet call for new subscribers was an editorial headed "The Roman Catholic Hierarchy: The Deadliest Menace . . . ." Catholic bishops and the confessional were his alternate punching bags for the next several years.

Two Catholics in political life were Watson's personal targets. Edward D. White was elevated to Chief Justice of the Supreme Court and Joseph P. Tumulty followed Woodrow Wilson from the governor's office in New Jersey to the White House as private secretary. Watson's caricature of Tumulty striving to adjust his halo was the least offensive of his cartoons. Three times the Department of Justice sought to have his journal barred from the mails. Watson's innate political knack was borne out when he was elected United States Senator in 1920.

That *Watson's Magazine* truly lived up to its claim of a national circulation may be doubted. But there could be no questioning the tremendous distribution of a weekly which gushed forth from the town of Aurora in the Ozarks of Missouri. In November,

1911, the Archbishops of New York and Boston were named to join James Gibbons in the College of Cardinals. The following month Wilbur F. Phelps took over the abandoned opera house of Aurora for publication of *The Menace*. The first issues were distributed free, but that was not necessary for long. Within a year the subscribers had mounted to 120,000, thirty times the population of Aurora, counting from the patriarchs to babies at the breast. Three years later this figure seemed insignificant when a million copies a week were loaded on every train out of this southwestern Missouri town. Steam engines coming in did not pull so much bulk but a load of more value. Envelopes not only brought the price of new subscriptions, but payments for the host of anti-Catholic books which were advertised profusely in *The Menace*.

Unlike other so-called "patriotic" publications, this Goliath of anti-Catholic newspapers had no target save the Church. Expanded circulation was reflected in the broadening of the volleys leveled against her. Early in 1913 a headline screeched "Romanists Run St. Louis." Late in 1914, when the sale of the paper had ballooned to almost 1½ million, the Vatican was so often the topic it would appear that *The Menace* had a staff of correspondents in Rome. Of course not even the price of a cablegram was wasted, for myths were more easily fabricated when undisturbed by truth.

PRIEST SUES

The Knights of Columbus aroused the ire of *The Menace* in appropriating $50,000 to investigate prejudice in the United States. A spurious oath attributed to that organization, apparently used for the first time against a member in a Pennsylvania congressional election, was frequently spread across the front page. Much like the false "Instructions to Catholics" fabricated by the A.P.A., K. of C. members were alleged to swear that they would butcher those not of the Faith. When the bogus oath was published in a national Catholic newspaper, *The Menace* mangled the truth by proclaiming its falsehood was copied from a "Romanist journal."

United States courts have decided libel laws do not apply to the Church or the Knights of Columbus as a body, however malicious and scandalous the charges. This broad interpretation was inapplicable when *The Menace* smeared the character of a West Virginia priest, who was awarded $1,500.00 for libel. It was the attorney for *The Menace* who declared that the newspaper was so notorious that its charges should be believed by no one! Testimony during the trial revealed that during the first six months of 1914 this "scandal sheet" earned $500.00 on each $100.00 share of stock. The honey of such profits attracted numerous ravenous flies. Sixty rivals bloomed forth, seeking to make stings against the Church in their newspapers the loadstone to riches.

A retired Congregationalist minister, Dr. Theodore C. (Daddy) Walker continued as theological advisor of the town's "best-known production." The more important financial control passed from Phelps to Billy Parker, erstwhile organizer of coal miners. Wine had no attraction for handsome Billy, but women and song soon were consuming most of the unaudited billows of greenbacks which surged into Aurora. Highways, or rather cross-state roads, were little traveled in those days, but the sides of boxcars, in addition to the multitudinous numbers, bore the persistent exhortation: READ THE MENACE. Unlike 19th-century forerunners, this journal did not urge its readers to tar and feather Catholics or to burn their churches. But wasn't so much pressure bound to produce an eruption? Blatantly proclaimed to be based on "facts" from *The Menace,* a rash of "convent inspection" bills were introduced in state legislatures from Vermont to Arkansas and from Florida to South Dakota. Inevitably Missouri had one, presented in the House by John H. Lehr, from a county near Aurora. In effect, it was tabled by the House Judiciary Committee, but a companion measure in the state senate afforded an opportunity for a member to launch a stream of slurs at the Church and her members. Having endured all he could, Senator Mike Casey warned that one more insinuation would bring personal action by himself. Poe's description of *The Raven* applied to the reviler: "Nothing further then he uttered."

A bit later in Ohio Representative Richard R. Hawkins introduced similar legislation. Before a vote was taken he made an unauthorized demand on the Convent of the Good Shepherd in Cleveland to search the premises. The Mother Superior telephoned Bishop Joseph Schrembs for instructions; the Bishop responded by coming immediately to conduct the tour himself. Representative Hawkins was so impressed that he at once had the bill killed in committee.

MENACE EXTINGUISHED

Meanwhile, as one writer has jocularly expressed, "the *Lusitania* had been sunk by a German U-boat, having no discoverable connection with the Pope." The most avid sensationalists were satiated with the war news. Subscriptions to *The Menace* declined, but Billy Parker's excursions to Kansas City "dives" grew more expensive with the H.C.L. (High Cost of Living), the phrase of the day. The heavily insured plant of the newspaper went up in flames as a sort of Christmas present to Catholics in late December, 1919. A skeptical insurance company refused to pay off in cash and forced Parker to rebuild. Hammer and nails could not restore the address plates of subscribers and *The Menace* started down the desolate road to extinction. But its fame—or infamy— was not extinguished immediately. According to Frank Peters in the *Springfield* (Mo.) *News & Leader,* a youngster in a White House receiving line blurted out: "Mr. President, I'm from the home of *The Menace.*" Warren Gamaliel Harding needed no amplification. He replied: "Oh yes, Aurora, Missouri."

Though the last gasp did not come until after his death, Cardinal Gibbons' judgment of 1914 was vindicated. The Archbishop of Baltimore then advised against Catholics endeavoring to have *The Menace* barred from the mails. Freedom of the press was more important to him than hastening a collapse which he foresaw was certain to come.

Before the corpse of *The Menace* was buried in the graveyard of anti-Catholic publications, almost a million American Catholics had helped bring World War I to a victorious conclusion. After presenting long lists of pacifist ministers of various denominations, a compiler stated: "I am informed there were one or two Catholic priests who were pacifists during the war, but I have been unable to find them." The same author, Ray H. Abrams, declared that there was not one case of a Catholic soldier being unsettled in his belief in God. Again America had seen that Catholics were the best of citizens!

Chapter XVIII

HATRED INFLAMED BY
THE KU KLUX KLAN

WHEN PRESIDENT WILSON SENT HIS WAR MESSAGE TO CONGRESS on Good Friday, 1917, the patriotism of the American people engulfed domestic differences of every type. A commission established by the Knights of Columbus to investigate religious prejudices was promptly dissolved. The concluding report stated: "The war will kill bigotry; not the individual sentiment but the movement." Looking beyond the military struggle to the days of peace, the commission foresaw that "following in the war's wake there will come . . . an overflowing feeling of human kindness, sympathy and understanding."

The optimism of the Knights is not to be criticized; a high regard for others benefits the possessor more than anyone else. Unfortunately for the realization of the hope expressed, an organization had been formed two years previously which was to enlist more members than any other anti-Catholic group in America. The official title: Invisible Empire, Knights of the Ku Klux Klan.

SLOW START

Such a name certainly was far more impressive than A.P.A. or Know-Nothing. Its deviser was William J. Simmons of Atlanta.

A private in the Spanish-American War, he called himself Colonel as he was alternately preacher for two Protestant denominations and salesman for fraternal societies. Designating himself Imperial Wizard, with a few comrades Simmons founded the Klan on Thanksgiving night, 1915. A wooden cross wrapped in burlap and soaked in kerosene was ignited to furnish a flickering light—the Fiery Cross! The garb of white sheet and vizored helmet may have been inspired by a stirring motion picture, "The Birth of a Nation," which idolized the Klan of Reconstruction days.

The Klan was closer to being invisible than imperial during the first five years, growing slowly to no more than 5,000 members. Then two adventurers seeking employment after the war sensed the possibilities inherent in the skeleton devised by Simmons. Solemn Edward Y. Clarke and plump Mrs. Elizabeth Tyler shoved fagots of publicity under the simmering cauldron. By a signed contract Simmons was to retain his title and $75 a week, but to Clarke came $8 out of every $10 Klecktoken (initiation fee). Toward the end of 1921 Clarke and Bessie Tyler were rich from the almost 100,000 members who had enlisted.

Apparent is the motive of these two promoters and the field agents with whom profits were divided. Whence and why came those who donned peaked helmets and white sheets? More mumbo-jumbo than any previous secret society and the alliteration of "K" attracted many Klansmen to Klonvocations. More than this was needed, however, to keep dollars rolling into the Imperial Palace in Atlanta. While anti-Semitism added some appeal, it was anti-Catholicism which injected the adrenalin. In the South a passiveness toward the Church had been changed to hostility by *Watson's Magazine* and *The Menace,* the two publications most successful in smearing Catholicity. As membership expanded northward to the rural Midwest it became identified in the popular mind with a heritage of Anglo-Saxon Protestantism. Ministers were admitted free, and itinerant preachers more than professional organizers became the propagators of the Klan.

NEW KLAN HEAD

During 1922 membership bounced upward at the rate of 3,500 daily, with a corresponding income of $45,000 every 24 hours. This was far too much to be intrusted to the idealistic Simmons. He was bought off and retired, to be replaced by a moon-faced dentist from Houston, Hiram Wesley Evans. To remove the stigma inflicted on the Order by investigations of the previous year, Evans dismissed Kleagle (organizer) Clarke. The help needed by the Evans factions for this upheaval was supplied by David C. Stephenson of Indiana.

The origins of Stephenson are obscure. His first emergence into the public eye was in the 1920 election, when he ran as a wet Democrat. Having been defeated by the Anti-Saloon League he followed the axiom, "If you can't beat 'em, join 'em," becoming a bone-dry Republican. Next he was Kleagle of the lone Indiana council of the Klan at Evansville. His salesmanship was so successful that soon he was given control of 23 states. So effective was he in Ohio and Indiana that each had about 500,000 Klansmen. It was to the Hoosier State that Stephenson finally directed his full attention. There his power became so tremendous that truly he could declare, "I am the law in Indiana."

Devoid of spiritual interest himself, Stephenson perceived that "old-time religion" was attractive to rural Hoosiers. Anti-Catholicism to him was merely a means of acquiring the money and power he craved. Under Stephenson's systematized direction control of the Republican Party was gained from every precinct or block to the very state capitol in Indianapolis.

About ten per cent of the population of Indiana was then made up of Catholics. However, they were concentrated in the industrial cities of the north. In many rural sections the faithful, being almost entirely unknown, were easily pilloried with almost any charge. A photograph of the beautiful Cathedral of the Episcopal Church, under construction in Washington, D.C., was widely circulated. The credulous readily believed the accompanying story that this was a palace being erected for the Pope, soon to move to the United States. When another rumor was circulated that the Pope would temporarily live in an Indiana town, 1,500 people are reported to have met the train on which he was expected in order "to take care" of the Pontiff.

STEPHENSON'S DOWNFALL

Monster demonstrations were frequently employed both to entertain the Klansmen and to bring pressure to join on additional thousands. "Steve" arranged his investiture as the Grand Dragon of Indiana for July 4, 1923, at Kokomo. In his own airplane he dropped from the sky to a waiting throng of 200,000. Garbed in a purple and yellow robe he apologized to the crowd for his delay, deluding his listeners with the claim of having been conferring with President Harding. Subsequently in Indianapolis Klansmen were disturbed by frequent guffaws emitted by the steed of a mounted policeman. Only later did some surmise that there might have been a connection between the "horse laughs" and the officer being an Irish Catholic.

"The Old Man"—as Stephenson liked to be called—revived the Horse Thief Detective associations. Under 19th-century legislation constables had almost summary powers, which were used in the 1924 election to gain information bringing office-seekers under Klan control. Being a Catholic, of course, immediately disqualified any candidate. Early on election morning "clothespin ballots" were thrown in front of the doors catalogued as receptive, the sample marking of candidates having been enclosed in a clothespin.

Almost as soon as Stephenson had seized supreme power in Indiana, the reins slipped through his fingers. In 1925 he was sentenced to life imprisonment for the death of a young woman he had criminally assaulted. Instead of the pardon "Steve" expected, in prison he was prevented from having contact with anyone, lest he divulge the corruption which existed.

The anti-Catholicism of the many he placed in public office oftentimes was as political as Stephenson's. When an Anti-Religious Garb bill was presented in the state legislature, Governor Ed Jackson telephoned Bishop Joseph Chartrand to give assurance it would never become law. One morning the attention of John L. Duvall, Klan Mayor of Indianapolis, was called to the traffic hazard at 14th and Meridian, where Catholic institutions were on the four corners. A traffic light was installed before noon!

MEMBERSHIP EXPOSED

Especially for businessmen the vizor of the Klan helmet was essential. Thereby benefits, real or imaginary, of membership were secured without arousing the ire of those opposed to the Invisible Empire. That protection was ripped away by a tabloid, *Tolerance,* published biweekly in Chicago. A roster of Klansmen having been surreptitiously obtained from the Indianapolis headquarters, issues promptly sold out when they contained names of members. Exodus from the Klan resembled the abandonment of a sinking ship. Even today librarians assert that it is almost impossible to retain copies of *Tolerance.* So-called researchers are prone to depart with the evidence of membership in the long defunct anti-Catholic organization.

Hoosier young men were not as easily befuddled as some of their elders. At the time hooded goblins were parading unchecked, Wabash College, Indiana's Presbyterian institution, had four Catholic students in an enrollment of 300. One of these was unanimously elected captain of the basketball team and another president of the student council. When the news reached the campus of Notre Dame University that four students had been badly beaten by Klansmen in South Bend, almost the entire student body roared the three miles to town. Klansmen were ready to repel them with sawed-off shotguns from the upper floor of a downtown building. Famous for his inspirational talks at half time, football coach Knute Rockne delivered the best of all. Still a Protestant himself at that time, "The Rock" persuaded the angry students to walk back to the campus singing with him the "Notre Dame Victory March."

Elsewhere, as in Indiana, the Imperial Empire disintegrated and eventually dissolved. After Atlanta was elevated to an episcopal see, the then Bishop Gerald P. O'Hara bought the former "Imperial Palace" in that city. The cathedral and parish school were built on the grounds and the "Palace" converted into a rectory. When the cathedral was dedicated in 1939, the Imperial Wizard of the dormant Klan expressed a desire to attend. Atlanta newspapers commented that the Klan, having been organized to make Mass impossible, came to its end by having the Imperial Wizard attend Mass.

Chapter XIX

CATHOLICISM AN ISSUE DURING 1924 AND 1928 ELECTION CAMPAIGNS

No AMERICAN COULD HAVE BEEN UNAWARE OF ANTI-CATHOLICISM in the 1920's! As the decade opened a fresh method of attacking Catholic schools was devised. During President Grant's administration a constitutional amendment had been offered against them; this time the avenue was through a sovereign state. In 1922 Oregon adopted a law whereby every child was required to attend a public school. While almost all the press attributed this law to the Ku Klux Klan, actually Scottish Rite Masons were the original proposers and sponsors of the measure.

UNCONSTITUTIONAL

Father Edwin V. O'Hara, later bishop and archbishop, enlisted aid to test the constitutionality of the Oregon law. The Federal District Court declared: "A compulsory school act could not be more effective for utterly destroying private schools if it had been entitled 'An Act to Prevent Parochial and Private Schools from teaching the Grammar Grades.' " The black cloud which hung low over Catholic schools was scattered by the United States Supreme Court ruling the law was against the Constitution. The fundamental right of parents to care for their children had been vindicated!

While this thrust was being successfully turned on the West Coast, a political star had risen in the East. This luminary was the Catholic governor of New York, Alfred E. Smith. By three votes out of more than 1,000 the Ku Klux Klan kept the 1924 Democratic convention from condemning the order by name for its religious bigotry. Then the delegates deadlocked over the presidential nominee. Imperial Wizard Evans claimed Smith's defeat was due entirely to the Klan. John W. Davis, the compromise selection, later condemned the organization, but the G.O.P. contender Calvin Coolidge refused to speak. "Silent Cal" unintentionally was the jokester of the year in stating that about his party's platform he refused to be a chatterbox.

During the following year the Klan ballooned to its maximum expansion of approximately 8,000,000. Thereafter the fetid air began to seep and then gush forth; membership catapulted downward to 321,000 in 1927 and to less than half the next year. Yet, as Hiram Wesley Evans boasted, the hooded order retained an intangible power, due, not to what it was, but what it might be able to do. The most raucous voice continuing to rasp forth was that of J. Thomas Heflin, Senator from Alabama. For two, three, four hours in the senatorial chamber he vented his spleen against Catholics.

"A LOOK AT THE RECORD"

In 1926 the tremendous progress of Catholicism in these United States was brought out by the Eucharistic Congress in Chicago. At the same time it furnished unlimited material for baiters of the Church. At a public reception in New York for the Papal Legate, Governor Smith kissed Cardinal Bonzano's ring. To Catholics this gesture was similar in other circumstances to a gentleman's tip of his hat or a serviceman's salute. Professional anti-Catholics, however, could scarcely have howled louder had the Governor produced a Communist membership card. Adna W. Leonard of Buffalo, Methodist Bishop and President of the New York Anti-Saloon League, publicly declared: "No Governor can kiss the Papal ring and get within gunshot of the White House. . . ."

Notwithstanding, a year before the convention Al Smith was far in the lead for the Democratic presidential nomination. In an open letter in the *Atlantic Monthly,* an Episcopalian attorney, Charles C. Marshall, queried: Could Smith as a Catholic uphold the Constitution in every respect? Answering through the same magazine, the Governor relied on a phrase he was to make nationally famous, "Let's take a look at the record." Nineteen times he had taken the oath of office in New York; the voters' persistent approval testified to his faithful execution. While newspaper reaction was overwhelmingly favorable to Smith, a comment in the Baltimore *Sun* penetrated to an underlying truth: "The people who believe that Catholicism is the enemy of Americanism will continue to believe it no matter how cogent the proof to the contrary."

A generation before Theodore Roosevelt predicted that the future would see "presidents who are Catholic, as well as presidents who are Protestants." Once the Democratic delegates had chosen the New York governor, Methodist Bishop James Cannon strove to confute this forecast. While stressing the prohibition issue, the Bishop did not hesitate to attack Catholicism. Perhaps more than any other single individual, Bishop Cannon was instrumental in breaking the Solid South, traditional bulwark of the Democratic Party.

Herbert Hoover's name had been placed before the Republican Convention by a zealous California Catholic, Joseph Scott. Subsequently, many of the faithful became critical of the Republican candidate because of his silence regarding anti-Catholic support. In extenuation it could be said that no one knew what the effect would be since it was the first national test for a member of the Church. Not so easy to understand is the statement found in Hoover's *Memoirs* (p. 209): "The religious issue had no weight in the final result."

Were this analysis correct, then a stupendous amount of effort and money was expended without impact. Space permits but a minute smattering of the abundant evidence that campaigners against Smith considered his Catholicism the vital factor.

MILLION-DOLLAR BIGOTRY

A former governor of a Midwestern state declared that it was impossible for Al to be at the same time a good American and a good Catholic. He urged the faithful in the United States to set up a church separated from the Pope. An Assistant Attorney General of the United States advised a convention of Methodist clergymen that they should tell their congregations to vote against Smith. Even the Chicago *Tribune,* an ardent supporter of Hoover, condemned this appeal to religious prejudice as "an act for which an official should be removed from office." But the official was neither dismissed nor ceased campaigning until election day on November 3.

A prominent North Carolina woman asserted that the anti-Catholic literature poured into her state must have cost a million dollars. One publisher's record of turning out leaflets and pamphlets against the Church went back to the American Protective Association of the 1890's. On one post card, of which he mailed thousands at the penny rate then in effect, he wildly claimed that a victory for Smith "means the Pope above the President, the Canon Law above the Constitution, and the Papal rag above the American flag." Another card addressed to women read: "I charge the

Pope with being 'The Chief of White Slavers.' " Before the writer is a four-page leaflet sent out by another publisher. Of the thirty reasons given for voting against Smith, more than half are calumnies against the Church.

It has been estimated that anti-Catholic newspapers were distributed in the astounding number of 5,000,000 copies weekly. Though they contained appeals for contributions, the papers were sent to anyone considered susceptible without waiting for payment. Stories too vile or indecent even for these "scandal sheets" were circulated by chain-letter systems. Libelous cartoons probably were even more effective, for the pictures made an impression upon those who had no intention of reading.

RESTRAINT OF CATHOLICS

When the head of the Women's Democratic Club of Baltimore appealed to the Catholic women of Maryland to support Al Smith, the Baltimore *Catholic Review* declared: "The Pope would not dare to make this suggestion . . . his suggestion would not be accepted if he did dare." The Associated Press widely quoted from a sermon of Archbishop John J. Glennon of St. Louis, the remark that: "The mission of the Church is the salvation of souls, not the election of Presidents."

On election day the New York *Times* deplored the religious controversy injected into the campaign. Conditions would have been far worse, the journal asserted, save for "the fact that Catholics have exhibited such wonderful restraint under attacks upon their Church. They have kept silent even in the face of notorious misrepresentation and calumny."

When the votes were counted five states deserted the hitherto Solid South and Smith was decisively defeated. Notwithstanding, the Catholic candidate received the highest popular vote ever polled by a Democrat, approaching the combined total of his party's candidates in the 1920 and 1924 elections.

If anti-Catholicism had been rampant, still there had been none of the violence whereby Know-Nothings in Baltimore drove Catholic voters from the polls in 1856. The fair-minded outside the Church, and especially the secular press, had learned that defamations long accepted without question were totally false. Most of all, as the New York *Times* recognized, the Church could be thankful that her children in the United States had refrained from returning evil for evil.

Chapter XX

CATHOLICS ADVANCE AS BITTERNESS LESSENS

THE DARK SOMBERNESS ASSOCIATED WITH NOVEMBER IN THE northern part of our country was, in 1928, in keeping with the dejected spirit of many supporters of Alfred E. Smith. Though three candidates divided between the two major political parties have since received fewer electoral votes, Smith's total of 87 was dishearteningly low. Some political analysts asserted that the Democratic Party was finished nationally, though it might serve a useful function in local contests. Even more positive were the assertions that no major political party would again make the fatal mistake of nominating a Catholic for the presidency.

SMITH "CRUCIFIED"

Everything from Smith's boyhood around New York's Fulton Fish Market to his affiliation with Tammany Hall were suggested as reasons for his defeat. Undoubtedly these were factors, but a delegate from the Texas which defected in 1928 proclaimed the consideration which others avoided mentioning. During the 1932 Democratic Convention in Chicago Maury Hughes declared: "They crucified that great American Alfred E. Smith on the cross of religious intolerance."

Yet in the very year of Smith's defeat there were more American priests than there had been American Catholics when George Washington became the first President. Nor did Catholic leaders vanish. James A. Farley and Edward J. Flynn directed the successful campaigns of Franklin D. Roosevelt. These New Yorkers were succeeded by "Bob" Hannegan of St. Louis, likewise a Catholic.

The Great Depression was the principal concern of most Americans during the 1930's. Unlike the panic of 1893, it incited no talk of Catholic immigration being responsible for the excess of job-seekers. After President Coolidge signed an immigration bill on May 26, 1924, newcomers from countries predominantly Catholic were severely limited. However, no restrictions at all were needed during the depths of economic collapse, years during which more people left our shores than sought admittance.

Thirty-one days after the Nazi panzer divisions swept into Poland and World War II commenced, President Roosevelt proposed sending a special envoy to the Vatican. Cardinal Mundelein of Chicago died that very day; to this churchman two years previously F.D.R. had first suggested our country's cooperation with the Holy See. Though some opposition immediately flared up, the President was not deterred. Pope Pius XII welcomed his Christmas letter that they work together for peace. Accordingly announcement was made of the appointment of Myron C. Taylor as the Personal Representative of the President with the diplomatic rank of Ambassador. Though peace proved distressingly elusive, in Rome Mr. Taylor assisted the Vatican in distributing money and supplies to the millions of war refugees. Taylor was not a member of the Catholic Church, yet he had entertained the future Pope in his home during the 1936 visit to the United States of Cardinal Pacelli.

EARLY DIPLOMATIC CONTACT

In the Roosevelt Papers at Hyde Park, New York, are many letters of praise to the President for his appointment, with a large proportion from those not of the Faith. This was by no means the first diplomatic contact. From 1797 the United States maintained consular representation in Rome. Formal diplomatic relations were established by President James K. Polk. These continued until 1868, when Congress failed to appropriate money for the expenses of our minister. In the 20th century William Howard Taft was sent to Rome to settle the problem of the Friars' Lands. This property was owned by religious orders in Spain, and with our acquisition of the Philippines the question of disposition arose. Consequent to the negotiations of the future President with Pope Leo XIII the lands were sold and the issue amicably adjusted without uproar.

The death of President Roosevelt and the cessation of declared war did not terminate the Taylor Mission. This personal representation continued until Taylor's health caused him to resign early in 1950. Late the following year President Truman nominated General Mark Clark as Ambassador to the State of Vatican City. A reading on the thermometer of heat generated may be found in the headline of the magazine *Newsweek*: "Vatican Furor!" A complication arose from a law of 1870 connected with the Peace Policy of President Grant, whereby army officers were forbidden to accept civil positions. Before any solution was reached General Clark withdrew his name. One critic of United States-Vatican diplomatic relations was incorrect in asserting "that our beloved Lincoln would not do such a thing," for the first Republican President actually made three appointments to the Papal States.

Long years before Archbishop John Ireland had pointed out

the Church "refuses her love to neither rich nor poor; but the poor are the majority of mankind, and her affections flow out more copiously in the direction of the majority." In cooperating with the Personal Representative of the President, the Holy See had amplified its paternal care of the most abject of the poor—the refugees of war.

PAUL BLANSHARD

The rapid rise of the Ku Klux Klan after World War I had temporarily splotched America's proud record of religious liberty. The pattern was similar after World War II but spread with less momentum. One method of undermining the respect of fellow Americans for the faithful was the so-called scholarly approach. The best-known practitioner has been Paul Blanshard. His writings and lectures have been copiously sprinkled with quotations from Church documents. Usually the wording was accurate, but the statements gave contrary implication by being adroitly abstracted from their original context. After all, twice in the Psalms appears the assertion, "there is no God." The scriptural passages may be rightly understood only when rejoined with the preceding words, "The fool has said in his heart."

Agitator Blanshard represented one phase of an organization formed in 1947. The lengthy title is Protestants and Other Americans United for Separation of Church and State, commonly abbreviated P.O.A.U. Frequently since 1957 the magazine *Christian Herald* had expressed dismay at the possibility of any member of the faithful being considered for President. A claim of objectivity was completely discounted by such statements as "Senator Kennedy would be an invaluable public asset if he were not a Catholic." The effect was apparent on a woman attending the P.O.A.U. convention in Boston during February, 1960. She reported that her Catholic friend had denied that the faithful hate all those outside the Church. Apparently in good faith the woman observed: "Catholic people do not even know their own religion."

Misapprehensions such as this woman suffered in most cases had their origin in time and place far distant. Most of them can be traced to a tainted heritage of a religiously divided Europe. Once the animosities were sharpened to support exaggerated nationalism or private greed. Like liquid still trickling in a slightly tilted aqueduct after its source has gone dry, these hatreds based on falsehoods seem to endure in America when they have been discarded in the lands of birth. In Germany Catholic Chancellor Konrad Adenauer drew enthusiastic support from Lutheran constituents. At the University of Fribourg, operated by the Church, this writer found hundreds attending from the so-called Protestant cantons of Switzerland without any dissension or animosity.

INHERITED TRADITION

If tensions in America have not lessened as rapidly, neither has the United States had more than four centuries in which to heal the cleavage. While the origins were identical for all those of European ancestry, is it not true that a transplanted plant sometimes has greater strength? In the thirteen English colonies survival was almost the sole hope of the few valiant Catholics. During the American Revolution they proved that oppression had not chilled the warmth of their love for a new homeland. Praise from George Washington was testimony that leaders of the fair-minded outside the Church recognized the extraordinary patriotism of the faithful.

During the 19th century the increasing number of Catholics irritated the badly disposed. Press and platform—and sometimes pulpit—were employed to transform ignorance of the Church and her members into hostility, all too frequently violently expressed. As Paul Simon, a contemporary Lutheran, reminded a group of

Wisconsin ministers: "Modern Protestantism . . . has inherited a tradition of militant, emotional anti-Catholicism."

Gradually in the last century and more rapidly after 1900 education has lessened the animosity toward the faithful. Improvement in the intellectual, economic, and social level of American Catholics inevitably scattered myths about them for reasonable fellow citizens. Intelligent people more and more have come to see that "ignorant" or "unthinking" did not apply to neighbors willing to make great sacrifices to maintain their own schools. Then, too, the exceptional valor of American Catholics against foreign foes or Communist infiltration rendered ridiculous any questioning of the patriotism of the faithful.

CATHOLIC RECORD

Over a century ago a Catholic church in Newark was attacked by a mob. On September 8, 1854, the New York *Tribune* commented that this was the fifth or sixth such outrage. The article continued: "There is no instance on record wherein a Protestant house of worship has been ravaged by Catholics." A hundred years and more have not besmirched that record. The advance which has been achieved by the faithful in the meantime has in great measure been due to the good will of those not of the Faith. Let our appreciation be shown to all by our being the best of American citizens!

With a Catholic President the responsibility of each of the faithful has increased immensely. Braggadocio on the part of even a few will not only make the position of the Chief Executive difficult but will react against every other member of the Church. If based on love of God and all of His children, active Catholicity will not become odious to anyone. The insignificant minority of faithful of 1776 won the commendation of our First President, George Washington. Under the first Catholic President every

Catholic must—and will—strive to win that tribute from fellow Americans who are not of the household of the Faith.